The Journal of Junk Culture & Fringe Media • Est. 1986 • Issue 52

Exploitation Retrospect

- 2 ...ongs and ...roform, ...uctions
- 24 Prose That Packs a Punch
- 32 The Destroyer: The Sun Source of Series
- 35 Remo Williams: The Adventure Begins (& Ends?)
- 36 Foot to the Face Cinema
- 44 Lancasterploitation
- 48 Review Section

EXPLOITATION RETROSPECT: THE JOURNAL OF JUNK CULTURE AND FRINGE MEDIA is published occassionally by Dan Taylor. All contents are copyright their individual authors.

Contributors to this issue: David Zuzelo, Jonathan Plombon, Chuck Francisco, Neil Burke, Mitch Lovell, CE Martin, John Grace, Jim Ivers, Doug Waltz, Jay Kulpa, Crites, Adam Knabe, Matthew Saliba.

Images are used for editorial purposes only and remain the copyright of their original owners.

On the Cover: Remo Williams and The Magnificent Chiun as imagined by illustrator Neil Vokes and colorist Matt Webb.

ER logo (originally debuted on ER #26 aka The Complete Guide to Klaus Kinski/Winter 1989) designed by Barry "The Evil Twin" Wooldridge.

Please direct all mail and items for review to PO Box 5531, Lutherville, MD 21094-5531. Electronic correspondence should be addressed to editor@dantenet.com.

Visit us online at www.dantenet.com, like us at Facebook.com/ExploitationRetrospect and follow us at Twitter.com/ExploitationWeb. Don't forget to read the ER blog at EROnline.blogspot.com.

A huge thank you to all of our contributors, both print and on-line, for making ER a reality since 1986.

Special thanks to (Damn You) David Zuzelo, Mitch Lovell, John Grace, Jonathan Plombon, Chuck Francisco, Neil Vokes and Matt Webb for contributions above and beyond the call of duty.

WET FINGERS, FOGGED DONGS AND SAPPHIC SLAPFIGHTS

A Penetrating Poke at Nikkatsu Erotic Films Collection Volumes 13-15

by David Zuzelo

I'm always up for a challenge when it comes to my choice of cinema. Give me your Baron Corvo films featuring midgets in sailor suits with blowguns chasing down babysitters to wrestle on a water mattress any day and I'll go looking for more. However, I have to admit to always being slightly squeamish when it comes to the Pink genre of Japanese Cinema. Maybe it's all the screaming and ropes and rape and sex that seems to constantly feature the moaned/belted out "Yamate" ("stop it"). I don't really know, but when you put something in front of me as the editor of this fine mag has done I just have to dip in...

I'M GLAD I DID, because installments 13-15 of Impulse/Synapse's NIKKATSU EROTIC FILMS COLLECTION are a wide ranging bag of screeching insanity, pure oddity and in one case, surprisingly affecting drama. Really. Reading this I want to make clear that I don't pretend to be an expert on these films, and there are many out there who could really give more insight to the genre as a whole. What I hope to do is share the perspective of someone new to the rope game of Nippon Naughty. Everyone starts somewhere... And while I have seen a lot of the 90s DTV action things, these are entirely different and my opinions definitely will have that new electro pussy shock crème smell to it (read on...)

So, with trembling hands I popped the first disc in (well, not trembling, but excited) and couldn't help but give Mo Fuzz a little love as I said, "Let's get in to trouble, baby." Surprising how well that fits these films. Because they are LOADED with maximum trouble.

First up... the film that met my expectations in both the best and worst ways... Volume 14!

SHE CAT (MENEKO)/1983
Directed by Shingo Yamashiro

Apparently, this is an unusually long entry into the Nikkatsu films, and sure does have a lot going on in here. I was amused to see the director's credit pop up over a woman's spread legs (and fogged vagina) as she is getting checked out a clinic. Indeed, this one is what I expected already! We meet two doctors working in a clinic for women, but our first patient up is Tommi, a drag queen pretending to be pregnant to get a goofy idjit in the waiting room to throw a party for her. The doctors go along with this happily, and already we are in to some questionable ethics as far as this clinic goes... but it gets better/worse as hoped. Kagami and Hiratsuka definitely end up in trouble as the party (which is actually kind of sweet in a bizarre way) is slashed short by machine gun fire from some underworld types that have an axe to grind with a missing skull (ohh...my head...) and hell breaks loose. The ladies need to get their agendas and plan straight, so in order to forget we can all enjoy a sensual shower sex scene. I enjoyed it plenty at least. But something ain't right here... flashbacks show us how the "she cat" name came to be and the two women have a bizarre dominant and submissive relationship going that we realize isn't going to survive the stress. Next thing you know we are at a cross dressing funeral full of snark, revelations to past gangster ties and oh yeah, an entire subplot that would make Dario Argento say, "uh...really?" involving facial reconstruction from a dead woman's apparently well cared for skull. And lets not forget the hand extension shower nozzle sex including much fogged penis flopping (I assume). That is probably the highlight of the film for me, as the couple goes from hot action to what I think is the actress chuckling as she gets blasted in the face while pretending to get rear ended.

Anyway, SHE CAT looks like an action picture by the artwork on the disc (though not on the artwork included on the Japanese poster in the insert), and it really is not at all. But it does feature Japanese thugs doing the things they do, and they do them with vigor. I can't say the overall sex appeal of the beautiful Ai Saotome really would make me forget the gang rape that takes place directly after a woman gets an abortion ("The way should be clear!") that goes on for several edits away from the scenario puts this in the overall "hot flick" category, but again SHE CAT feels exactly as I expected these to run.

But that isn't entirely bad either. I found the evil dominant doctor Hiratsuka fascinating as a character. She has some bad ties obviously, and she flips on her friends and is ready to commit murder to cover up her tracks before the 90 minutes are over. Morality is a bit quirky in Nikkatsu films to my experience, and none more than hers. She hops into bed with an old work cohort who has her terrible past at her fingertips after he tries to rape her as she moans, "you are still a bad boy aren't you?" She obviously has a lot of affection for Cat, but when she can't manipulate her or those around her the gloves come off and that femme goes fatale. Heck, in this film they all go that way.

Enjoyable? Sure, though the scorecard keeping nature of the plot through me a bit, but I can't help but appreciate the crazy level of mixed elements that make the film work as a whole. There are some parts that stroll around like a stray cat, but overall...it's a fine pussy of a tale that prepped me for more and never made me want to tie myself up and wail YAMAAA-TEEEEE!!!

And the gun on the logo does get a little play, there is a fine shootout that almost matches the blissful intensity of all that water nozzle ballistic bathtubbery.

WITH THAT post-abortion gangbang quota met, I move on to what I think was the best of the batch... a film that shocks, surprises and sells me on the fact that I really do need MORE of these films. It's time for some...

FEMALE TEACHER HUNTING (ONNA KYOSHOI-GARI)/1982
Directed by Junichi Suzuki

A young couple make out in a pool as some ominous music plays (and damn fine ominous music it is) and a mysterious voyeur watches them. They manage to show off some truly abysmal "sexy" kissing skills, but that is not why the music is being ominous. No. What we just saw was a false rape about to be reported and our young lead, Daisuke, is in deep crap in his boarding school. The accusation sends him into a sputtering rage against his beautiful teacher (to be hunted) and he even goes to the girl he was with for a little "rough seduction" as Nikkatsu men are wont to I guess. The clever trick here is that all the students are gone and he makes his gal announce over the PA system how great a lover he is (it starts with all the NO NO NO all of these encounters do of course)... and it's genuinely distressing to say the least.

Drifting away from academia, Daisuke finds himself in a small village where he is just another victim instead of a predator, until he is taken in by a tattooed vendor and his ultra horny wife. What he couldn't expect is how different the sex he was having in school would be from this very twisted adult edition that has now sucked him into it's grasp. He unwittingly at first serves as a sex aide for the couple, both to satisfy the wife's desire AND to keep his new male role model as "the hardest he's been in some time!" While that scene plays out in an excruciatingly awkward yet erotic manner, the real payoff, and the thing that sets FEMALE TEACHER HUNTING apart from films like SHE CAT, is the outstanding performances as Daisuke finishes his part and tries shamefacedly to avoid the gaze of his male host. It's genuine and honest emotion amidst the chaos. And it doesn't stop there. Oh no.

The "Female Teacher" also arrives on the scene, but in a different way. The purported moral compass of the piece is desperate to meet with her married lover as he plays with his children on vacation in another example of complex sex situations for adults...so different from late night pokes in the pool. Another fine performance really gives depth to the role of Sakatani, the emotionally crippled (and eventually demolished) school teacher. The two forces collide once more and as one is dropped off into near madness, the young student finds his way back to school to realize that his vacation has now given him an education in more than mischief as he solves the mystery of his accuser and gets revenge by dominating those that he has felt wronged by, both male and female in an intensely bleak emotional finale that recalls the work of Jess Franco in the early 70s as the humiliated becomes the hunter and the hidden dark corners of the psyche are either mastered and enacted or lead to ultimate disgrace.

My expectations were more than met by far in the brief 66 minute running time of this film for sure, it's got some unbelievable turns, some intense sleaze and also some incredible direction, sound and acting. If anything has sold me on exploring this world of weird social subjects and wet crotches with a side of fog it was this. There is a lot to dig in to, and one particular bit stands out when I explain how well constructed this is. And just how strange the culture of the movies can be. A man cumming on a woman's stomach is used twice in the film, exploring how sex can be similar in action, but different in meaning with an ease that I found shocking. Daisuke is urged on by his hostess to cover her in the "proof" of his desire so that she can see it, while Sakatani looks down as her married lover chides her for getting an abortion as he deposits his fluids on her and leaves her to wipe it up.

This is a film that is twisted on the surface, twisted underneath and elegantly told at the same time. Essential, this is what I was hoping for...

THE FINAL FILM IN THE LATEST WAVE left me scratching my head and chuckling... have you ever wondered what the charmingly idiotic American comedy 9 TO 5 would have been like if Dabney Coleman had been relentlessly finger fucking Lily Tomlin until she vaginally squirted all over his hands as Dolly Parton stumbled on the scene?

Me neither.

But, it happens, sort of, in HORNY WORKING GIRL: FROM 5 TO 9. And best of all, I did not know what they were parodying right until the VERY end because I had a bizarre cable TV flashback in the last scene since it looked like the poster for that comedy. Hey, I can spot a Franco film, but those Dolly comedies? Not so much.

HORNY WORKING GIRL: FROM 5 TO 9 (ONNA SHIN NYUSHAIN: 5-JI KARA 9-JI MADE)/1982
Directed by Katsuhiko Fujii

Opening on one funky ass groovy boobadooooooooobadoooo tune, the new girl arrives at the office to meet her horny boss. Chieko knows what she wants and just how to get it I guess, and the office workers may be jealous, but she doesn't care. Promising to broker a big deal for her new employer, it all gets sealed over some overt sexual tension naturally. But the more we learn about her, the stranger she is. She gets involved with fake deflowerings (with some VERY hilarious English language shenanigans by the way), perverts and purveyors of pussy shock crème. Uh, yep. You read that right. She isn't just ambitious, she's a HORNY WORKING GIRL, dammit. One minute we have mashers and maniacs, the next...on to erection special effects and sexy masturbation. Oh, and lets not forget the naked slapfights mixed with surgically repaired hymens. Yes, there is a lot going on here, and in an amazing compressed space. The boss is just so damn horny that the secretary, the long suffering wife and the HORNY WORKING GIRL will be united in anger and take that shock crème to town on one very lucky horndog. It's a cock shocking climax with an after dinner mint of a revved up Japanese man licking his own HAIRY FUCKING ARMPIT in some kind of lusty motion. With tongue. Extra tongue.

There is a lot of stuff to recap, but it's best to just watch and stare in awe to be honest, because while none of it is shocking, it is a surprisingly raunchy little sex comedy of Nikkatsu morals, shocking square ups and surprisingly wet fingertips.

And let us not forget the utterly distasteful violent rape sequence that brings the gals together! I don't think that was in 9 TO 5 (what a way to make a living in Nikkatsuville)...from that to women playing cock paper scissors for who gets to read an artificially stimulated hard on in under 70 minutes? It's just mind wobbling!

This one is actually recommended highly for Japanese skin fans in particular, the completely sexy Junko Asahina and her cohorts are beyond easy on the eyes and perhaps a strain to the male zipper (just watch in underwear I guess) and there is a manic humor to the entire thing that feels so wonderfully alien to me that I'd watch it again just to shock the crap out of any romantic comedy aficionados I may encounter.

Overall... a nice after dinner mint to the transexual funerals, the belly blopped semen, the shock crèmed clitorises and abortion clinic roughness these films presented. And all of this was under 4 hours.

So here is what I can take away and share with you regarding the Nikkatsu Erotic Films Collection from a tiny sample. If you want to see some astonishingly different films from most other trash cinema, it's a great start. The transfers are very solid, outshining the Impulse/Synapse SCHOOLGIRL REPORT discs with ease and valuable signposts to understanding the mayhem are offered up by Jasper Sharp in liner note form as well. You'll also get a glimpse at the brain clonking trailers for the movies, which are an art form unto themselves! (See the ER website and blog for David's ongoing coverage of the SCHOOLGIRL REPORT series.)

Impulse/Synapse offer a trailer disc by the way, but after watching the films I decided it would be best to avoid for now, there are so many turns and images (I mean, what the hell is that couple eating dinner while doggy styling away in the Impule opening?), why spoil anything??

As a dollar value I think it's a very mixed roulette wheel... but I'm willing to try and find some more unique and distressingly entertaining entries in this series for myself. Got a strong stomach and yearn for large nippled women with astonishing liquidity in the crotch? Come on down and get up to date with some of the sleaziest shockers you'll likely find on DVD. I'll bring the cock shock crème!

David Zuzelo is a full-time father, part-time Joe D'Amato Porn Excavator and non-stop Media Mangler. He has been writing about stuff for over a decade online and you can peek into his slightly unhinged brain by pointing your webmind at David-Z.blogspot.com. Print-oriented readers can pick up his co-authored book TOUGH TO KILL: THE ITALIAN ACTION EXPLOSION or just try and find some of his comics work in ZOMBIE TERRORS or A.K.A. if you dare! Lamberto is his favorite Bava.

Looking for more Nikkatsu coverage? Be sure to check out the ER blog at eronline.blogspot.com and the ER website at dantenet.com for complete coverage of additional installments from Impulse!

McFarland

People hunting people for sport—an idea both shocking and fascinating. This book examines in-depth all the cinematic adaptations of Richard Connell's iconic short story.

THE MOST DANGEROUS CINEMA: People Hunting People on Film

BRYAN SENN

296 pages $45 softcover (7 × 10) 50 photos, notes, bibliography, index
Print ISBN 978-0-7864-3562-3   Ebook ISBN 978-1-4766-1357-4   2014

800-253-2187 • www.mcfarlandpub.com

A Camcorder,
Some Chloroform,
The Story of
WAVE Productions,
and an Underground
Culture of Death-Fetish Films

In 1987, a math teacher named Gary Whitson opened Whitson's Amateur Video Entertainers, a production company built on the mantra to make horror films that wouldn't skip the deceptions, stabbings, and everything else that could be considered "good stuff." Whitson's do-it-yourself mentality, assisted by that decade's ever increasing affordability of camcorders, served as the foundation for a catalog of films that now ranges from KIDNAPPED AND CHLOROFORMED AGAIN to DROWNED DAMSELS AND WET T-SHIRTS. Over 25 years since its inception, Whitson's WAVE – now known as Whitson's Audio Video Entertainment – continues to satisfy the cinematic bloodlust of fans everywhere. Fans who are as much of the story as the films are.

But no matter how you look at it: the fans, the kidnapping, the cannibalism, the hillbilly stew from the film HILLBILLY STEW. It's WAVE. The little company that could – can and does. It started small and it still is today, a rebuttal of sorts to the overblown spending of Hollywood.

"[The crew] is basically me and whatever actors or actresses that are needed for a particular production. I do the editing, much of the writing and most of the camera work as well as sometimes appearing on camera," he explains. "This is an extremely low budget operation."

A small budget that works to his advantage.

"The budgets are small so a profit can be earned quickly and because I don't spend a large amount of money for things in the movies," Whitson says. "I don't want to be put in a position of spending a large amount only to have the sales not justify it."

Nonetheless, Whitson has still been able to land a number of notable names for his shoestring conveyor-belt movie-making including scream queens Tina Krause, Laura Giglio, and Tracey Lixx. These lung-expanding luminaries have all graced the WAVE's greatest films, flaunting knife-wielding that would shame Michael Myers and retire Jason Voorhees.

One former WAVE actress, Pamela Sutch, who stars in films WATER GAMES 2: DEADLY VENGEANCE and WITCHFINDER 2, thinks that working for the company helped her grow creatively, especially when it came to shooting a personal favorite of hers, QUICKSAND AT DEADMAN'S

article by Jonathan Plombon

CREEK.

"We had an outline of a script [for QUICKSAND AT DEADMAN'S CREEK] and ended up improvising most of the story as we went along," Sutch remembers. "The best and most natural acting most often comes from improvising."

Since working for WAVE, Sutch has begun Siren Tales Productions, her own production company which has developed a best-selling series of transformation titles where men are turned into women and the old are turned into the young. One of the films, TRANSFORMED, was co-written by Sutch.

"I became very comfortable as an actress and writer for the reason of being able to improvise in so much of WAVE's work," she says.

Another WAVE regular, who could arguably be considered the face of WAVE since 1994, is Debbie D. Her history with the company is so extensive that even she has no idea the true scope of her contributions. She's been in over 100 WAVE films.

"WAVE movies are always fun to make," she says. "You never know what will take place and there is always a lot of jokes and laughter."

Much like with Sutch, it's been a learning process.

"Gary Whitson is very laid back as a director and takes whatever you offer him. In the beginning I wasn't up to par so I was on my own with developing my character and becoming the actress I am today. I am very thankful to him for all that on screen practice," Debbie D. says.

Perhaps the most appetizing ingredient for WAVE's success is, ironically, the intentionally bad-taste plots. Anyone's stomach has to both growl and squirm at a film like THE KIND OF MEAT YOU CAN'T BUY IN THE STORE, which concerns a detective named Barefoot Jenny (Carol Livingston) who is hot on the trail of a dealer specializing in human flesh. Another, EATEN ALIVE: A TASTEFUL REVENGE, deals with Stacey (Debbie D), an executive in a cosmetic and fashion company who finds out that she lost her promotion to her roommate Lisa (Tina Krause). Stacey exacts revenge by building a shrink ray, which she uses to turn her boss (Sunny), as well as her roommate, into bite-size, easily digestible morsels.

Where do these ideas come from? A good portion are pulled from the minds of WAVE's fans. For around $300 to $2500 and higher, an approved script can be custom made with everything that their blackest heart's desire.

"At least half of our library consists of custom tapes. The fee charged covers basically the expenses and any profit comes from sales. I used to do custom artwork in the '70s and '80s and I figured I could also offer custom tapes and make money from it," Whitson says. "People often want things that they can't get in a mainstream horror movie."

The custom-tape feature has also become a staple of some of WAVE's associates. Sutch's Siren Tales Production provides custom-tape work and actress Laura Giglio has become well-known for her series of made-to-order mermaid videos.

While Whitson contends that the reason why fans pay WAVE to produce their script is because they want to "see their vision on the screen," it's not just horror junkies plopping down a paycheck because they want to see their nightmares come to life. Many of WAVE's films are discussed on death-fetish forums and sold to death fetishists. Death fetishists are individuals who watch videos of simulated murder for sexual arousal. This underground market thrives on forums where these videos are commissioned and sold.

Highly secretive even on their websites, death-fetish producers have been active for decades where they practice extreme confidentiality and shy away from any publicity. One producer, who wishes to remain anonymous, explains why.

"The secrecy is because we are misunderstood... it is not so much our fear, but the fear of the 'normal' folk who would assume that we are a dangerous element in society because of the misconceptions that naturally flow from the very phrase 'death fetish'," he says.

The Producer explains what a death fetish is.

"The erotic female death fetish consists of the visualization of a female's death in a fantasy-only setting which contains elements that the fetisher finds sexually stimulating. These fantasized elements can vary from one fetisher to the next, but the most common elements are a beautiful, desirable woman usually dressed in a sexy fashion who suffers from a fatal attack and dies in an erotic and unrealistic fashion," The Producer reveals.

Furthermore, he stresses it's the simulation that makes the fetish.

"Realistic death scenes are seldom part of this fetish, because real death is not pretty and in fact is quite ugly. The fetisher does not hate women or want to punish them," he says.

A death fetish video can vary from one to another. All the films, though, have a common thread: a woman is attacked and killed. How the death is portrayed, and the extent of the content, depends on the video. Some simply depict a death scene, while others include XXX aspects where the murderer commits sexual acts on the body before and after the woman's demise. Some acts are even more popular than others. Chloroform and strangulation have a large following.

The Producer explains the place of women in a death-fetish video.

"A beautiful and desirable woman is indeed sexy and her image on screen is a sexual object. The impacting of a beautiful woman with a phallic symbol, or the domination of such a woman by strangling her, does have a sexual element, because one is fantasizing about exerting some manner of control over that woman, and the ultimate type of control is death," he says.

He believes it's the influence of tinsel town.

"When our actresses die, they die in Hollywood fashion, maintaining their beautiful looks throughout. Fetishers are fascinated by a beautiful woman being killed or dying, just as the general public are fascinated fifty years later by the death of Marilyn Monroe in her prime. We fetishers find it hard to get our heads around the fact that a once beautiful and vibrant woman is now a cooling corpse," he says.

The question remains, how does a death fetish develop?

"There are several theories, but the one that I personally subscribe to is the theory of imprinting," The Producer says. "It appears that most fetishers can trace the first stirring of these fantasies back to puberty. When these individuals were trying to understand their emerging sexuality, they were exposed to female death scenes through some type of media, including TV, movies, comic books, and pulp magazines. These scenes involved beautiful women who these children were beginning to find desirable, but they were killed, often with phallic symbols such as knives, guns firing bullets in a fashion not unlike ejaculation, or in a tight embrace resulting in strangulation. Somehow, the child's mind connected the act of screen violence with the sexual act."

Some death fetish videos do differ from WAVE. Unlike the death-fetish videos, WAVE occasionally balances the images of murder with strong female characters who get the upper hand on their assailants.

"WAVE has an entire catalog of strong character type women in their movies. I mean — did you forget that I played Rana, Queen of the Jungle? And how about FEMALE MERCENARIES ON ZOMBIE ISLAND where I took over the entire world? And there was also PSYCHO SISTERS where we cut off — you know," Sutch says. "WAVE has a well rounded diversified variety of horror, comedy, action, fantasy and hot women movies."

However, WAVE doesn't hide from content geared towards the death-fetish community. Its website sells compilation tapes like WAVE's ASPHYIXIATED CLIPS VOL. 1, WAVE's DROWNING CLIPS, and WAVE's QUICKSAND CLIPS.

"I would categorize [WAVE's films] as death-fetish videos," The Producer says. "Gary sometimes categorizes them as horror films. Well, since slasher films probably created a lot of death fetishers, maybe it is fair to categorize them as such."

"I don't target them specifically," Whitson says. "I shoot the movies basically the same way I did when I first started back in 1987 way before there was any 'death-fetish' community unless you consider people who watch horror movies part of that group."

Another death-fetish producer, who also wishes to remain anonymous and will be referred to as The Insider, has been working in the industry for 18 years. A movie connoisseur from the onset of adolescence, he attended film school but ended up in the death-fetish circuit watching his fellow students struggle to finish their own mainstream movies. For him, the death-fetish films also need to be properly defined and named. A better term, he believes, should be "fantasy erotic death fetish."

"The movies are ultra violent. But I make them because I enjoy seeing how intense and violent I can make it look with all kinds of actresses at different levels of skill. Everything is, of course, fake. So, while there are those outside the community who might look at the finished product and be disgusted, I look at the project from a directors-editors standpoint. I don't see violence, I see acting," he says.

And the violence can be almost anything, since the death fetish covers many sub-fetishes. For example, shooting is a main category, but then that's broken into sub-genres that include where the bullet is shot, with what type of gun it's shot with, and how the woman reacts to the shot. If she's breathy, gaggy, noisy, or noiseless all factors in to what the customer might want and what might become a sub-fetish.

Plot also plays a big role. Although it's the death scene that sells the film, it's the story that death fetishists use to become emotionally connected with the death. Something as simple as an explanation as to why the man is invading a house can have an impact on the selling of the video. Is he jealous of a new boyfriend? Did she steal something of his? Even with the custom videos, Whitson won't accept anything — and that includes just images of a woman hurt.

"I don't take scripts that are just about beating someone up. It's got to have a beginning, middle, and end and must have a reasonable plot. I've turned some down, but the customer usually knows the criteria we go by before asking for a custom," Whitson says.

"I would say less than 1/8 buy for the beating torture scenarios — probably far less," The Insider reveals. "Most are just buying for the death scene, the postmortem scene and they all like a little set up. Plot is more important for certain types of videos."

T he market for these videos encompass a large variety of individuals. According to The Producer, women, as well as men, make up a good deal of fans. The Insider has even sold his videos to people one would think would be unlikely to watch them. It's the fans that The Insider thinks is one of the biggest misconceptions of the community.

"[The biggest misconception] is that [the customers] like real death. That they are messed up somehow. That they are anyone other than your fathers, sons — even daughters and mothers — postmen, bankers, policeman, judges — yes, I had a state Supreme Court judge — actors, musicians," The Insider says."You would not believe the famous people."

Actress Debbie D., a veteran of death-fetish videos, admits to never having a problem with any producer she's ever worked for or meeting any of the genre's fans.

"I think the fans I have met are super down to earth people. Some of the nicest people I have met have had a death fetish — let's face it — it's fantasy," Debbie D. says.

Then there are the mainstream filmmakers whose films might reveal a glimpse of their own death fetish.

"I have been asked to recreate such scenes as Hitchcock's PSYCHO shower scene and FRENZY strangulation," The Producer says. "It is strongly suspected that Hitchcock and other famous directors did indeed have an erotic death fetish."

Death-fetish actresses can be practically anyone. Some begin as models and introduced to it by producers. WAVE recruits a great deal from horror conventions. Some are adult stars. The Insider's company will pay a model around $150-200 an hour to appear nude in a film, while performing hardcore could raise the rate to around $300-400 an hour. A female porn star can make $3000-5000 for 2-3 days work.

Then there are scream-queen actresses, like Debbie D., who have made a career in the death-fetish circle without performing sex on camera.

"At first I didn't know I was making death fetish movies. I was getting custom work and doing it. I was than being hired by other companies from my experience and popularity," she says.

Debbie D. is a producer's favorite. Much of which is probably due to her attention to detail and the lengths she's willing to go to give a performance

"I am usually the one who wants to take it as far as it can go. I have even tried real hangings three times and it hurts like hell, even days later," she says. "My vocal training has allowed me to do breath holds under water for long periods and I try and do a very tight throat squeeze [during drowning scenes]."

WAVE and the two previously mentioned producers aren't the only individuals in the industry. Others, like Seductive Studio and adult actress Rachel Steele shoot their own custom-made death-fetish material for customers. They openly sell their content on their websites.

"We produce some death fetish because that is what our customers request in their custom videos. We try to think of it as producing a movie, much like Hollywood would show death scenes in their movies, and not try to focus on the actual act, but on the actual script or film," Seductive Studio says.

While not every film they've made has been released on SeductiveStudios.com, they have produced over 1000 films with some of their most popular videos being JUSTICE GIRL BETRAYED and BOOTED BEAT DOWN. For Seductive Studio, they're just doing what tits big-brother, big-budgeted brethren do.

" I would have to say that Hollywood and our culture in general perpetuates violence. Not just in women," Seductive Studio explains. "We believe in freedom of speech and if you don't like something you don't have to watch it. Our fans, I hope, can tell the difference between reality and fantasy. The majority of our films you could see at the theatre."

Adult star Rachel Steele has made a career out of delving into taboo topics including video content that simulates incest and, of course, death, for her website at RachelSteele.com. It started as a request from fans. Now it's part of the website's everyday content with 300 death-fetish films available to subscribers.

"It doesn't turn me on to be strangled or to watch somebody being strangled. Or to see blood or to see someone gasping for air. Or eyes rolling back in their head," she says. "But those are all the detailed requests that I get. They're very detailed. They want to see tongue sticking out, eyeballs rolling back, eyes fluttering."

For Steele, many of her ideas come from cable.

"I can see how some of this content would be disturbing to some people. But then you have to realize too, I've gotten ideas by watching TV shows. Like, 'oh, that would be a good one!' So it's there, it's already happening. I'm just bringing nudity into it, really," she reveals.

Although it takes only a camera and a couple of people of actors and actresses to theoretically to enter the industry, it's a little harder to sell the product to customers. Steele has had to use a website vender from outside of the country, which has made it difficult to maintain the site

"We're having trouble finding a venue where the credit-card companies will allow us to sell the content," Steele says. "This is where hypocrisy comes in. You can see this stuff on TV. And the only difference is that we're showing actual intercourse."

Others have had to deal with the same problems. In 2001, President George Bush struck a deal with credit-card lobbyists for incentives if they'd go after producers making content they didn't approve of. It's something that has affected the Insider directly.

"This started the war on fetish," The Insider says. "BDSM was the major target, as was extreme fetish, which is our kind of stuff, I guess. Credit-card companies put 100s of 1000s of mom and pop operations out of business. The policies still stand today with most TOS on credit card billings stating what kind of content is not allowed. Basically, they decided to censor people."

The Insider points out that one of the largest points of profit for credit card companies is hotel porn.

"It's made it a pain," he says. "If not for that, I would actually be doing well, and not stuck in a house I desperately want to move my family from as the neighborhood goes downhill."

While some death-fetish producers struggle, WAVE still manages to carve out success in a spot between the death-fetish community and the mainstream horror world, allowing the small studio to develop further. A comic-book division called WAVE Komix, which will issue graphic novels based on WAVE character, has just launched. On the video front, he'll be remaking SLEEPOVER MASSACRE and FEMALE MERCENARIES.

"Since I'm now 65, where WAVE is now is fine," Whitson reflects. "In fact, it's what I worked toward since the '90s. I wanted to build a library of movies that I could continue to sell basically forever and be able to cutback as I got older, but still be able to shoot occasionally. And now with downloads, I have a whole new group of customers who are purchasing the movies."

No matter the year. No matter the trends. WAVE proves that there will always be a demand for drowned damsels and wet t-shirts.

And hillbilly stew.

Jonathan Plombon is a frequent contributor to the pages of Exploitation Retrospect both on-line and in print. He previously wrote about the Porn and Wrestling Connection for ER #51 and you can find his reviews of recent DVD titles throughout our review section beginning on page 48 as well as at dantenet.com.

"THE MOST FEARSOME CREATURES IN THE TRANSGRESSIVE CINEMA." ROGER EBERT

"A WALK ON THE WILD SIDE."
THE NEW YORK POST

"ABSOLUTELY EXCELLENT!"
DIAMANDA GALÁS

"YOU CAN'T CALL YOURSELF A GENRE FAN AND NOT OWN *DARK STARS RISING*. IT'S JUST THAT GOOD."
THEATER THOUGHTS

"A WHO'S WHO OF THE MOST BELOVED VISIONARIES, TRAILBLAZERS, SUBVERSIVES, AND FREAKZOIDS OF THE PAST 50 YEARS."
FILM COMMENT

"*DARK STARS RISING* IS A TRUE NECRONOMICON, A BLACK BIBLE OF TRANSGRESSION & TRANSCENDENCE, OF THE OTHER AND THE BEYOND."
BEYOND HOLLYWOOD

"FANS OF THE DARK, DEMENTED, AND DEPRAVED SIDE OF CINEMA, REJOICE — SHADE RUPE HAS WRITTEN YOUR BIBLE."
HORRORVIEW

TURA SATANA + CRISPIN GLOVER + DIVINE
TELLER + GASPAR NOÉ + JIM VANBEBBER
ALEJANDRO JODOROWSKY + UDO KIER
FLORIA SIGISMONDI + RICHARD KERN + CHAS. BALUN
RICHARD STANLEY + BUDDY GIOVINAZZO + DAME DARCY
HERMANN NITSCH + PETER SOTOS + WILLIAM LUSTIG
BROTHER THEODORE + GENESIS BREYER P-ORRIDGE
DENNIS PAOLI + JOHANNA WENT + ARNOLD DRAKE + JOHANNES SCHÖNHERR
ANDRE LASSEN + STEPHEN O'MALLEY + DENNIS COOPER + THE TORTURE KING

A BOOK BY SHADE RUPE
DARKSTARSRISING.COM

WEIRD WONDERFUL WORLDHEADPRESS.COM

Vintage Mags, Books, Toys & More
@ DansFunkyFinds.com

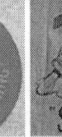

ER #52 :: page 15

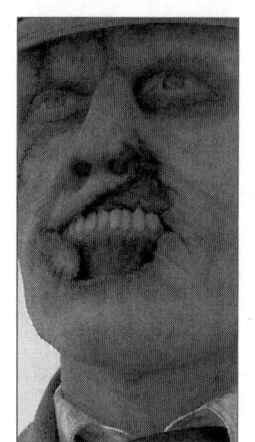

Criminal Decapitation of a Can't Lose Concept
When Killing Zombie Nazis Just Isn't Enough
By Chuck Francisco

If pressed to name a flavor of movie villain against whom you'd harbor no reservations inflicting catastrophic bodily damage, Vegas odds heavily favor your selection of either Nazis or Zombies. I can't fault that natural flash of neurons; among the annals of cinematic history there is no more wretched a creature than genocidal storm troopers of the Third Reich or the rotting meat popsicles which used to be friends and family. And there's nothing more satiating to the appetite of a splatter obsessed gorehound than the well-earned cracking sound of zombie skulls mixed with the righteous fury of Nazi evisceration. And so it's incredibly strange that the Nazi Zombie sub-genre suffers weaker representation than cake-loving fatties on the Soviet Olympic swim team...

ER #52 :: page 17

HOW COULD IT TRANSPIRE that this peanut butter and chocolate horror dream team accounts for less than twenty films over seventy years of cinema? Perhaps the truth is rooted in the quick, cash-in quality of a substantial proportion of Nazi Zombie flicks. SHOCK WAVES is irrefutably an absolute classic, approaching horror masterpiece status, and the far more modern DEAD SNOW evokes a bloody good time even as its legacy grows, but you'd find yourself hard pressed indeed to name five more. Given the exploitative nature of this monster mash up, Nazi Zombie films are possessed of a proclivity toward weak execution and barrel bottom scraping budgets. To uncover the fungal rot which infests this sub genre, we require a better understanding of the growth history.

The beginning dawned on the unsuspecting cinema going public in 1943, as they attended the talkies to take their minds off of the all too real horrors of World War II. Escape could be gleaned in the wicked personage of John Carradine, whose repertoire of maniacal scientists included a jaunt as voodoo zombie researcher Dr. Max Heinrich von Altermann in Monogram Pictures' REVENGE OF THE ZOMBIES. The evil doctor plies his craft in an attempt to supplement the Fuhrer's army with mind-controlled voodoo zombies. His insidious machinations would have seeded the world into the shade of a second dark age, if he hadn't succumbed to the mysogynistic desire for total dominion over his wife. Even in her zombified capacity she resists his commands, marshaling her fellow undead to effect the downfall of Dr. Nazi, S.S. The mad scientist and spy plots were wrapped around the zombie shenanigans like bacon on a scallop because the studios felt that the undead alone couldn't carry a film (ironic, no?). REVENGE OF THE ZOMBIES is certainly worth a watch for historical context, and for the excellent climatic scene, but is pedantically pudgy around the midsection.

I imagine a very young Mike Mignola, creator of Hellboy, watching the next film in this sub genre's evolutionary chain as a boy. 1966's THE FROZEN DEAD is decidedly different than REVENGE OF THE ZOMBIES, being twenty years removed from the latter and surfing atop the post voodoo zombie wave of the future: the reanimated dead. Nazi scientists keep the heads of prominent Third Reich leaders on ice until such time as their nightmarish experiments empower them to graft these malfeasant melons onto new bodies (think THE THING WITH TWO HEADS, only with more genocide and little mustaches). The effects are campy and laughable as a disembodied head controls phantom limbs via conductive brainwaves, spurring on grisly demises.

A decade long lull in the action follows, as the horror world adapts to the post-Romero zombie. NIGHT OF THE LIVING DEAD was a Mike Tyson force punch that rocked the delicate sensibilities of the American moviegoing public, shifting their complacency forward a mile, but forcing them to live among the horrors of film (as a mirror for the real world atrocities of Vietnam). Along the way through the loosey-goosey 70s, spook shows had begun adapting a camp quality (predominantly in the slasher genre), perhaps as a coping mechanism for this harsh reality. Apparently everyone failed to inform director Ken Wiederhorn, as he crafted an undead atomic bomb to shame FAT MAN AND LITTLE BOY.

1977's SHOCK WAVES would prove to be the nourishingly infectious fountain from which all of this era's Nazi Zombies imitators would reanimate, but to which most would reek in comparison (until the modern resurgence). Sustaining on a meager budget of one million dollars, SHOCK WAVES could easily have been earmarked for irrelevance, but instead worked every corner of development like a five star cinematic pimp; making everything work for its money.

Aging genre stars John Carradine (playing a

cantankerous pleasure boat captain and back from his stint being revenged upon by the dead) and Peter Cushing (as a viciously scarred former Nazi commander turned island recluse) are leveraged to tremendous effect and surrounded by a competent cast of mixer fodder. The location scout also deserves tremendous accolades, as the hauntingly creepy use of the beached concrete steamship SS Sarpona lends SHOCK WAVES iconic gravitas, and the abandoned hotel belies the decrepit nature of Cushing's reclusive existence. The zombies are a Third Reich experiment which took aim at creating the ultimate, unkillable aquatic commandos. The resulting monstrosities became violently uncontrollable and, at the conclusion of World War II, were purposefully sunk in Cushing's sealed cargo hold near tropical Bimini. Rather than assail our visual cortex with rapid flashes of out of focus zombies in dark corridors, Wiederhorn lingers on his ominous undead. His long takes of them slowly, knowingly advancing, simultaneously breaks from established tradition and inspires tremendous dread.

SHOCK WAVES WAS WELL RECEIVED enough to inspire the capitalist fires of exploitation, which would see producers shovel a number of progressively boring titles down genre fans' throats. 1981 seemed to be The Year of the Nazi Zombie Film, during which no less than three such schlocky cinematic hor d'oeuvres were dished out (as of print it remains the year most flush with them). First came director Jesus Franco's OASIS OF THE ZOMBIES, which boasts some entertaining zombie-on-tank action, and a smattering of titillating flesh-ticuffs, but is tediously paced, and dangerous viewing if

you're already quite sleepy. The film is a regrettable use of a cool concept – treasure hunters close in on Nazi gold protected by the zombies of Hitler's Afrika corps – completely under realized by an otherwise talented director.

Following quickly in its grave is the (clam) saucy ZOMBIE LAKE. If you've ever wondered what SS soldiers would do after reanimating at the bottom of a French countryside pond inhabited by nubile local girls keen on playing splash-fight, naked as they day they were born, this is your film. Ashamed director Jean Rollins (under the pseudonym J.A. Laser) aims his lurid aquatic camera directly up at the ladies' love canals, refusing to break (brown) eye contact as the teens scissor kick away, completely oblivious to the dangerous undead leering below. ZOMBIE LAKE is a snore-fest, only memorable for its cheeky premise and naughty shenanigans. And my inner twelve-year-old will never forgive me for writing that.

Rounding out the crop of corpulent Nazi Zombie films from 1981 (and possibly responsible for snuffing out the burgeoning sub genre's unlife) is NIGHT OF THE ZOMBIES (not to be confused with the deliriously enjoyable HELL OF THE LIVING DEAD). This boring investigative drama has Nazi Zombies tacked-on as a cash-in afterthought, and with less than five minutes of on-screen zombie action, your time is better spent watching gore montages on YouTube.

After the Atari-esque market crash of master race undead films, there wouldn't be another seriouss treatment of the material until 2006. That

ER editor Dan Taylor blows his chance at a Parent of the Year Award by holding his 7-day-old daughter next to the DVD menu of her first film – ZOMBIE LAKE.

doesn't mean enterprising filmmaker Krishna Shah wouldn't try to spice up the proceedings with a rock & roll horror adventure populated by dwarves, sex perverts, hicks and Hitler. The deep-fried drive-in nature of HARD ROCK ZOMBIES transformed it into a video store legend, sought out by all devout teenage trash cinema archeologists of the early 90's. The plot (stretched into a feature length film from a short created for the film AMERICAN DRIVE-IN) follows a heavy metal band who happen upon a FOOTLOOSE-styled town full of hicks that fear all forms of music. In their infinite inbred wisdom, they murder the band, paving the way for their resurrection as KISS-styled zombies hellbent on saving the town's children for metal. Why does it warrant a mention here? It just so happens that an aging Adolfo Hitler has taken up residence in the town, and once the not-so-gentle folk are slain by the band, they also return as pallid shamblers. This is truly schlock to its core, but HARD ROCK ZOMBIES stood as the last bastion of Nazi Zombie celluloid until the early 2000's (PUPPETMASTER 3 is sort of an odd case which I've purposefully omitted).

THE 1990'S STAND OUT as a black hole for quality zombie films. The odd pocket of diamonds hidden amongst otherwise unmemorable undead cinema (CEMETERY MAN, for instance) was largely passed over for campier fare by moviegoing audiences. When the dam of zombie media finally broke anew with 2002's 28 DAYS LATER (yes, I know they aren't technically zombies) and 2004's DAWN OF THE DEAD remake, an unstoppable content flood of biblical proportions rained down upon an eager population, who still cannot get enough rotting apocalypse baked into their over stuffed entertainment pies. And while that storm may soon wane, putting zeds back on the shelf for another decade, we've gotten a number of Nazi Zombie mash ups in the meantime. Owing to the fact that we're now so far removed from World War II, a weighty number of these more recent films are period pieces, while others deal with folks who stumble upon long shuttered Nazi experiments.

The purposefully unremarkable HORRORS OF WAR would light the fuse, exploding with the kind of phony drive-in style which so infuriates old school schlock fans, but which is an inevitability of the film making system that currently holds sway. An independent production released in 2006, HORRORS OF WAR takes place behind enemy lines during World War II, where several American special ops soldiers have been tasked with discovering the truth behind Hitler's secret weapon (hint: it's zombies!) and put a stop to it. This fizzles in nearly every way, getting the modern wave of Nazi Zombie films off to a less than auspicious start.

Hot on its heels, 2008's OUTPOST takes a number of distinct liberties with this well-worn slant. Set in modern times, a corporate scientist hires a band of mercenaries to escort him to a scuttled Nazi bunker in some far flung Eastern European country. Once there the true scope of Hitler's terrible atrocities are writ personal, as the extra dimension Nazi Zombies take the crack soldiers apart piecemeal. The pseudoscience takes generous inspiration from HELLBOY, which is not a bad spring to drink from. Making successful use of a meager budget, OUTPOST succeeds at being the first good, serious film of the subgenre since SHOCK WAVES thirty years earlier.

Less than a year later, the Queen of Nazi Zombie cinema to SHOCK WAVES' king exploded on the festival scene. DEAD SNOW came to American audiences from that new bastion of quirky horror: Norway. Set in a cabin cresting a snow-bearded mountain, this energetic gore comedy struck the kind of gold that so many cheapie, independent, faux-exploitation films blow their O-ring attempting to emulate. A group of medical students plan a week's vacation of drinking, drug smoking, and snow sexcapades at the rustic cabin. When they accidentally stumble upon a box of Nazi murder gold under the cabin's floorboards, it awakens an entire platoon of vengeful, goose-stepping undead, bent on bloody satisfaction. DEAD SNOW is EVIL DEAD MEETS BRAINDEAD, with all of the hilarious gore and glee such a comparison conjures up. Occupying the trophy case spot as the Second Best Nazi Zombie film only due to SHOCK WAVES' classic status, DEAD SNOW may one day succeed the king as tastes and preferences transform.

What remains is a bevy of secondhand titles, clamoring for the gruel dripping from the edges of the table. 2011 period piece WAR OF THE DEAD looks visually impressive, and has strong practical zombie make-up, but languished through a nearly eight year production cycle, during which it lost leading man James Van Der Beek. It's by no means a poor film, rather simply an unexceptional entry amongst a slew of unremarkable movies (DEAD SNOW and SHOCK WAVES withstanding). Where it to have stood out phenomenally in any regard, WAR OF THE DEAD could have lorded over the roost, instead it becomes simply another decent way to spend a sleepless night.

A direct-to-video sequel to OUTPOST entitled OUTPOST: BLACK SUN was released in 2012 in Great Britain, but has yet to see (legal) availability stateside. There seems to be viable sustainability for the production company in this model of 3 million dollar movies as a second sequel, OUTPOST: RISE OF THE SPETSNAZ, is forthcoming. As to the quality of these derivative home market photocopies, I cannot yet speak.

EVEN FURTHER OUT ON the cusp of reality is the perpetually in production THE 4TH REICH, which was slated to meet the eyes of man back in 2011. In the space since, prolific actor Sean Bean has been added to the cast, which I'm certain will equate to a lavishly constructed on-screen death for the former double 0 agent. With the addition of Sex Machine himself, Tom Savini, I'm cautiously optimistic about THE 4TH REICH's potential, but given the history of the subgenre, the odds aren't favorable.

Sadly, the sub-genre which should explode off the pages of *Fangoria* festers like pig guts left in the sun. A bloated, rotting finger points at the cause, leveling the protruding bone at the perceived exploitative nature of Nazi Zombie films. This isn't the truth though, as many other absurd movie monsters have received respectable treatment in quality films through the decades. The reason horror aficionados are blessed with so few Nazi Zombie films is because early on they were established, by and large, as completely awful trains wrecks; boring films based on a cheap concept, with few upsides to their record. Piss poor treatment by incompetent filmmakers looking for a quick buck managed to derailed an entire burgeoning subgenre before it ever had a chance. That's tantamount to cinematic criminal negligence in my book. Perhaps the next generation of them will fare better. The history doesn't paint a hopeful picture, but at least we'll always have Bimini.

Chuck Francisco is a columnist and critic for Mania, writing Wednesday's Shock-O-Rama. He is a co-curator of several repertoire film series at the world famous Colonial Theatre in Phoenixville, PA. An avid beer brewer, rock climber, and video gamer, you can hear him drop nerd knowledge on the weekly podcast You've Got Geek.

Since this article was submitted, the Nazi Zombie Genre has continued to provide inspiration for filmmakers and entertainment for trash cinema fans. We're hoping that Chuck will take an opportunity to revisit the topic for a future issue or one of our online entities.

LIVE HARD

I remember *exactly* where I was when I first became aware of men's action novels...

It was the latter half of the 1970s and I had accompanied my Mom on one of her shopping trips. Despite being an occasionally over-protective parent – for some reason both KISS (ok) and for a brief period anything PLANET OF THE APES (huh?) were considered off-limits in our house – she had no qualms about planting me in the book and magazine section of the grocery store when we would do the weekend supermarket circuit. Ironically, I credit those hours spent thumbing through the paperback tie-ins of AUDREY ROSE and the original THE OMEN for my then-blossoming interest in trash cinema.

But when we ventured – as we did on this particular night – to the Moorestown Mall, she would let me hang at the independent bookstore that sat outside Sears and across from Roy Rogers. Located at the end of the one of the mall's arteries of commerce, I'm pretty sure it had one of those "clever" non-chain names like The Book End. And I can picture it like I was there yesterday. (Or so I'd like to think.)

As you entered the store, a magazine rack dominated the left hand wall while the checkout counter anchored the right hand side. A long two-sided rack/table ran down the middle of the store and that was where I first saw it.

Ostensibly under some kind of unspoken order to browse what Mom considered "safe" (anything STAR WARS or, surprisingly, James Bond) and avoid the big boy smut covered in plastic (which looked a lot like the mags hiding beneath piles of INSIDE SPORTS in my older brother's basement pad), I nonetheless would roam the store checking out the various paperbacks that were unlikely to land in the Scholastic Book Fair's offerings. I didn't dare pick up the sexy Western shenanigans of something called "Longarm" nor did I make much of some guy named Remo and his Oriental sidekick. Or was he a henchman? Maybe a teacher? *Oh, I had so much to learn.*

I would loop the long rack, stopping every now and then to thumb through a horror flick tie-in (how I wish I'd bought them all!) or make sure Mom wasn't walking through the door as I glanced at something POTA-related. Or worse.

But during one loop that night I spied a guy who looked a bit like Dean Martin waving a gun in front of a building that resembled – no, wait, IT IS! – Philadelphia's City Hall! Glancing around quickly (I'm sure the cashier pegged me for a filthy pre-teen shoplifter) I grabbed the book off the shelf and stared at the cover as I read the title out loud. "PANIC. IN. PHILLY."

Guys that looked like the old dude from the (alleged, ahem) mob family up the street lurked in the background while the Dean Martin guy took aim. All the while a curvy chick in flowered pants gazed lustily. As my brain registered that this book took place not on some made up planet or fictitious town (like Bayport, home of the Hardy Boys) but right across the river in Philly I flipped to the back and saw that The Executioner's travels had taken him to actual towns all over this great land – San Diego, Washington, Miami, Chicago, Vegas – where it appeared that he blew the living shit out of cars, buildings and people on a regular basis.

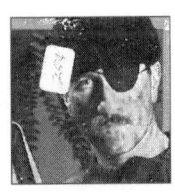

I desperately wanted to know *why* there was a panic in Philly and I was pretty sure it had nothing to do with a cheesesteak shortage. More importantly, I wanted to know what The Executioner planned to do about it.

But Mom showed up and that put the kibosh on all that. And, for some reason, that kernel of interest in men's action novels lay dormant for oh... three decades. Sure, the topic would pop on occasion and I'd laugh when Christopher George referred to Robert Ginty as "The Executioner" and I absolutely dug going to the multiplex and watching Fred Ward and Joel Grey banter away during REMO WILLIAMS: THE ADVENTURE BEGINS, but I never dipped into the swirling ocean of men's action until a few years ago.

Things came together – as they often do – in a perfect storm of interests and opportunities. My interest in modern horror was waining while my interest in modern (and not so modern) action was gathering steam. Trips to events like ActionFest (RIP?) featured conversations with card carrying Men of Action like John Grace who tipped me to the best – and worst – of the paperback genre. Excursions to used book sales, flea markets and thrift stores yielded hauls of titles like THE CHAMELON, SWAG, THE PROTECTOR, THEY CALL ME THE MERCENARY, THE EXECUTIONER (yay!) and the series that inspired the Remo Williams movie I loved so much. Barbecues and meet-ups with the one and only David Z left me staggering with boxes of mercenary tales, Mafia bloodbaths, spy shenanigans and other pulpy prose.

In other words, I was hooked. And, hopefully, after reading the appreciations of manly cinema and paperbacks that follow, you will be too... welcome to the world of **Blood, Brawls & Bullets**. – DT

FACING PAGE: Detail from Gil Cohen's cover art for THE EXECUTIONER #15: Panic in Philly.

Prose That Packs a Punch

DIRTY HARRY #1 : DUEL FOR CANNONS
by Dane Hartman

After three flicks cementing Spaghetti Western vet Clint Eastwood in the role of San Francisco Homicide Inspector Harry "Dirty Harry" Callahan, the versatile actor/director declared that his relationship with the .44 Magnum-brandishing cop was over.

Looking for ways to wring more cash from one of their most bankable creations – and establish their own line of men's action novels to rival Pinnacle's stars like The Executioner and The Destroyer – Warner Bros. launched 'Men of Action' featuring original Dirty Harry novels alongside such pulpier titles as The Ninja Master (see page 29), S-Com, The Hook (a "gentleman detective with a talent for violence and a taste for sex"), and Ben Slayton: T-Man.

Ghost-written by pulp and non-fiction vet Ric Meyers under the pseudonym "Dean Hartman", the first Dirty Harry adventure seamlessly flows from silver screen to printed page. Mimicking the beats and pacing of the original films, DUEL opens with a bloodbath at a cheap California amusement park as a hired gunman hunts down San Antonio sheriff – and Friend of Callahan – Boris Tucker. Though misguided officials would blame the deaths of Tucker and some local teens on the stressed Texas cop, Dirty Harry knows better and heads to the Lone Star State to settle the score.

Texas isn't very welcoming to Harry, with corrupt cops, local businessmen, street gangs, muscle-bound hit men and two-bit hoods hassling him at every turn. The SOBs even go so far as to slice up Harry's wardrobe and keep him from getting a cab. Soon, Callahan finds allies among Tucker's few remaining friends on the force – as well as a rival determined to kill him by book's end – and they look to disrupt the corruption flowing through town.

It's no surprise that Meyers – who also helped write DESTROYER #25: SWEET DREAMS (see page 30) – nails what we'd come to love about the Dirty Harry flicks, from Eastwood's mannerisms and fighting style to his minimalist dialogue. The book's cover art does nothing to suggest Harry isn't Eastwood and there's little attempt to describe him from a physical standpoint, so Meyers takes every opportunity to make you think Clint is delivering each pistol blast and flying fist during DUEL's many action scenes.

Though the tale veers dangerously close to going wildly over-the-top and is a bit too neatly wrapped up (a common problem with men's action tales of the day), DUEL feels more like a legit Dirty Harry installment than SUDDEN IMPACT (1983) or THE DEAD POOL (1988) featuring Liam Neeson (as a horror film director) and a pre-stardom Jim Carrey. Meyers' attention to detail and inclusion of characters and events from DIRTY HARRY (1971), MAGNUM FORCE (1973) and THE ENFORCER (1976) go a long way towards drawing us into this cinematic world.

DIRTY HARRY #1: DUEL FOR CANNONS landed on bookstore shelves in 1981, the first of a dozen entries in which "The Magnum Enforcer" would battle corrupt cops, serial killers, "dope-running sea pirates", terrorists, arms dealers (see DIRTY HARRY #10: THE BLOOD OF STRANGERS on page 27), a renegade government scientist and a killer looking to frame Inspector 71. The books can currently be found on thrift store shelves, flea market tables and boxed up at garage sales near grandpop's musty back issues of PLAYBOY (and the occasional OUI). – Dan Taylor

CHAMELEON #1 : THE WRATH OF GARDE
by Jerry LaPlante

Were James Bond to head up Q division the resulting hero might be something like Vance Garde, a "mild-mannered, scientific engineering genius" who uses his brains and the resources of his firm to, well, not so much *fight* crime as exact revenge against those he feels have wronged him and/or his family.

Garde intially leaps into action when his young stepsister Sharon dies of a drug overdose thanks to a low-rent dealer nicknamed "The Oregano Kid". Spurred on to "don't get mad... get even", Garde creates a division known as VIBES (Vindication against Injustice, Bureaucracy and Ensconced Stupidity) and enlists the help of the beautiful Ballou Annis to ferret out the upper rungs of the drug pushing ladder that killed Sharon. Along the way he uncovers clues to the identity of his father's murderer, experiences multiple bouts of blue balls with Ms. Annis, and dis-

GOING HOME and SURVIVING HOME are the first two novels in a new survivalist/post apocalyptic series by an author whose pen name is Angerey American. I would go as far as to say, however, that they are more like parts one and two of the same novel. The series has continued with the volumes ESCAPING HOME and FORSAKING HOME. **(WARNING: Mild spoilers for GOING HOME in the SURVIVING HOME review.)**

GOING HOME: Following an event that kills the majority of electrical goods from cars to microwave ovens, Morgan Carter must walk the two hundred and fifty miles home to his family. Along the way he runs into trouble and meets several allies with whom he faces the breakdown of civilisation as we know it. In an instant America (if not the world) is plunged into the Dark Ages and people soon turn on one another. Those desperate enough will kill without a second thought for an old loaf of bread. Those wicked enough kill and rape just for the hell of it. Luckily, being a keen survivalist, Morgan is more than ready and has his Get-Home bag in the boot of his car, a pair of good walking boots on his feet and a Springfield XD in his waistband.

Over all it was a good read, a self-published novel that had a couple of grammatical and spelling errors but nothing that pulled me out of the story. It grabbed me from page one and didn't let go; a thrilling adventure full of action, humour and character-building moments. There were a lot of abreviations and acronmyms involved, however, and some of them were a little jarring (there is a nifty glossary in the back of the book).

At times Morgan comes across as cold-blooded and a bastard (almost trigger-happy), and the first violent encounter he has really shocked me. The main support cast consists of his travelling companions; Jess, a naive young woman; Thad, a man-mountain of a truck driver; and, Sarge, a former military man who is straight-up R. Lee Ermey. These characters, thrown together by unimaginable events quickly become a family of sorts. They argue, they fight, they make up, they protect one another. As events progress it becomes clear that everything is not how it seems and maybe there is something else going on other than the EMP. It turns into a sort of conspiracy and really kicks things into high gear.

All things considered, even with the grammar problems and speling mistakes, (and the fact that the book has MASSIVE chapters – something I'm not the biggest fan of), I would still give this book a solid four stars out of five due to a gripping plot and brilliantly realistic characters with their own ethics, flaws and worldviews.

SURVIVING HOME: Surviving Home picks up immediately after GOING HOME. Morgan is back home with his family, trying to keep them safe in the face of growing adversity within his neighbourhood. This novel also has a greater role for Thad with him being – for all intents and purposes – the second main character. His story is followed in third person while Morgan continues to be his own narrator. The supporting cast for this book is also much bigger; Morgan's friends Danny, Rick and Mark each have their own character arcs. Whole chapters are dedicated to Sarge and his army pals fighting the good fight against the tyranical Department of Homeland Security who are rounding people up and shoving them into work camps againt their wishes.

Friends turn on friends. Neighbours turn on neighbours. Thieves, murderers and militias run rampant with wild abandon. The action dial is cranked up even higher. The dangers the characters face even at home are more intense and after the world-building and scene-setting of GOING HOME, the sequel is much more bleak and gritty. In places it is dark and unforgiving. Thad's arc here is especially messed up – I won't spoil it for you but it's Nasty with a capital N. It's messed up. It pulls no punches. Eventually events lead Morgan, Thad and Sarge back together as the DHS push on with their terrifying plans and it ends on one hell of a cliffhanger that teases all manner of good stuff to come.

SURVIVING is better wrote than GOING HOME – though it still has a few niggling grammar and spelling errors – and it's even more thrilling and adventurous with the promise of violence and fear hanging over every scene. Much like with GOING HOME, I would give SURVIVING HOME a rating of four stars out of five.

Now, if you'll excuse me, I'm off to prepare my own Get-Home bag and stockpile beans and rice. – *Neil Burke* penses with more than one villain in colorful fashion that would make James Bond blush.

Little more than "Bond Lite" but with more graphic sex and rougher violence, THE WRATH OF GARDE is a breezy read thanks to Zebra's typically easy on the eyes font size and the check-your-brain-at-the-door plotline. You'll figure out most of the twists and turns long before the "brilliant" Garde but you won't hate yourself for going along for the ride.

The cover copy and art might actually be more entertaining than the book itself. The artist's rendition of Garde (resplendent in white jacket and burgundy turtleneck!) appears to be modeled after a young Tony Curtis, though my wife suggested that there might be a little MANNIX-era Mike "Touch" Connors in there as well. As for the sheet-covered Ms. Annis? Sure looks like a hot young Liz Taylor to me.

More challenging than figuring out the artwork origins is deciphering the cornucopia of pop culture references used to sell the reader on the book, not to mention the most perplexing of all questions: Why the hell is this series called The Chameleon?!

Both The Incredible Hulk (?!) and James Bond (okay) get name checked on the back cover copy while there's even a reference to NETWORK's Howard Beale ("Like You, He's Mad As Hell And Not Gonna Take It Anymore!") that appears atop all three books in the series. The colorful "Chameleon" logo is prominently displayed all over the covers despite the fact that – as Marty McKee keenly points out at his blog Johnny LaRue's Crane Shot – "[he] isn't a master of disguise or a cat burglar or anything like that".

Alas, the adventures of Vance Garde and Annis Ballou never really caught on and the series ended after two more books – IN GARDE WE TRUST and GARDE SAVE THE WORLD. – *Dan Taylor*

SWAG #1: SWAG TOWN
by LS Riker

The United States has fallen victim to economic terrorism through a small-scale war conducted with assassins' bullets and a flood of foreign currency. By the time the "war" is over, the haves had fled to Europe and the shelter of their foreign bank accounts. The have nots have been left behind, old scores are being settled and payback – as you may have heard – is a bitch.

While the rest of America struggles under the belief that things will somehow be as they once were, New York City has become a playground for loads of skeevy Eurotrash and foreign jet-setters, a bustling center of commerce where anything – and everyone, it seems – is for sale.

Into the midst of this post-financial-apocalypse comes Swag, a former NYC detective who was shoved off the force in the aftermath of a bungled high-profile case. Swag – whose nickname is a mean-spirited joke and whose real name we never discover – is now forced to play bodyguard for the rich jet-setters who come in to the city and use their foreign cash to go on extended shopping sprees. But when one of Swag's clients gets blown away in a brazen, broad daylight hit the ex-cop wants answers... like who would want the pretty blonde dead so bad and what kind of hired trigger has Kevlar implanted *under* his skin?

Author LS Riker keeps the story moving as Swag drifts through the NYC underground – and briefly into Jersey – encountering low-lifes, mobsters, gun experts, hustlers, government men, ambitious bodyguards and a bevy of almost-indestructable killers who insist they are simply tourists. Even when they're trying to blow our hero's head off. (I couldn't help but be reminded of Mr. Gordons from THE DESTROYER series.)

SWAG TOWN seems more ambitious than your typical action novel of the era. Riker's NYC is familiar enough that you recognize it but *just* scary enough that you'd never, ever want to go there. Jam-packed with colorful characters and inter-weaving, overlapping plotlines, it requires a bit more attention on the reader's part than, say, the blast 'em all heroics of Mack Bolan – more than once I found myself doubling back to make sure I was making the right connections. (More on Bolan in ER #53.) Better than that, it never quite went where my expectations were leading me, which kept the novel full of surprises, from the financial war start to the action-packed finale.

Swag also stands out as a character, because unlike Bolan, Remo Williams, Nick Carter or other heroes of these pulp adventures he has no special training aside from his time as a cop and he is most decidedly human and vulnerable. On more than one occasion our hero finds himself in an impossible scrape, only to have his ass pulled from the fire by a character who may be a friend, a foe or a little bit of both.

Unfortunately, the Swag series only lasted for two more books: a Most Dangerous Game riff called FULL CLIP (1992) and the "more powerful than crack"-fueled revenge tale KILL CRAZY (1993). Frankly, I think Danny McBride should get himself in shape and option the Swag novels for his own action franchise. For some reason I kept picturing a blend of Kenny Powers and a MARKED FOR DEATH-era Steven Seagal as the Hawaiian-shirt sporting, pistol packing bodyguard hero of the novel. – Dan Taylor

DIRTY HARRY #10: THE BLOOD OF STRANGERS by Dean Hartman

While the first original Dirty Harry novel – DUEL FOR CANNONS (see page 24) – benefitted from the ghostwriting of Ric Meyers, the genre vet had to pass on certain installments due to his commitment to other "Men of Action" entries like The Ninja Master (written as Wade Barker). DIRTY HARRY #10: THE BLOOD OF STRANGERS is one of those installments and Meyers' deft touch with the material is definitely missed.

Even for a longtime fan of the original films, DUEL felt like an authentic Dirty Harry film adventure ported over to a pulpier environment, right down to Meyers' descriptions of fight scenes and our hero's sparse dialogue hissed through clenched teeth. STRANGERS – authored by Leslie Horvitz (THE DONORS, DOUBLE BLINDED, THE DYING) – feels more like a generic men's action novel whose main character just happens to be the beloved Dirty Harry. A suitably Eastwood-esque mug graces the cover but the man on the pages inside could be any random cop who gets mixed up in a terrorist plot funded by a Middle Eastern arms dealer.

In a terrifyingly lax pre-9/11 San Francisco, a couple of terrorist scumbags blow up part of an airport terminal and off some nosey patrolmen, which naturally draws the attention of Dirty Harry. But things get a little hard to swallow when our hero gets plucked off the streets to go undercover as "Dan Turner", a fill-in bodyguard for Gamal Abd'el Kayyim, a suspected arms dealer visiting California. After Harry/Turner foils an assassination attempt he finds himself moving in Kayyim's inner circle just as suspicion about him begins to boil over.

With every cop that could potentially ride shotgun either killed off or mortally wounded, Horvitz gives Harry a partner/love interest (of sorts) in Ellie Winston, anchorwoman-turned-reporter (Patricia Clarkson would play a similar role in 1988's THE DEAD POOL). Though it's hard to believe a seasoned San Francisco reporter wouldn't know who Callahan is, Winston finally realizes there might be a story in him and follows the cop from San Francisco to LA, Beirut and El Salvador as Harry's cover is blown and he finds himself matching wits and weapons with international arms dealers playing for both sides.

Brimming with head-exploding violence, THE BLOOD OF STRANGERS is a quick but instantly forgettable read. Whereas Meyers "gets" Callahan and the beats of the original films, Horvitz's attempts at harnessing their vibe fails and jamming Harry into international locales like Beirut and an Italian villa feels forced and more suited to an installment of The Executioner (more on *that* fella coming in ER #53).

After twelve "Never before published or seen on screen" novels the Dirty Harry series (pulp division) ended with 1983's DIRTY HARRY #12: THE DEALER OF DEATH in which Harry's beloved .44 Magnum is stolen and used in a series of murders intended to frame the cop. After seven years away from the character, Eastwood agreed to once again strap on the badge of Inspector 71 for 1983's SUDDEN IMPACT and, coupled with the fizzling men's action market, that meant the end of the books.

Though I'd certainly recommend other men's action books of the era over this one – particularly this issue's cover boy, the Warren Murphy/Richard Sapir creation *Remo Williams: The Destroyer* – the couple Dirty Harry novels I've tackled have been quick reads and brought back fond memories of a character I spent many hours with over the years. I'll certainly be keeping my eyes peeled at garage sales and thrift stores, hoping to grab installments where Harry battles filthy pirates, watches a family reunion go south, or has to clear his name. – Dan Taylor

NICK CARTER, KILLMASTER #31: MACAO by Manning Lee Stokes

Nick Carter, Killmaster, was not the first American attempt to emulate the trademark spy adventures of Ian Fleming's creation James Bond 007, but if NICK CARTER, KILLMASTER #31: MACAO is any indication, it may be one of the best. At least in terms of hitting all the right notes.

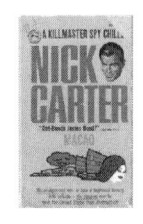

Carter – Agent N3 of AXE, a super secret and lethal spy agency of the United States – is a suave ladies man who is vacationing in London when he comes to the "rescue" of the out-of-control Princess de Gama, a Portuguese beauty with a dark secret in her past that she medicates with drugs, booze and the attention of the opposite sex. Or, as AXE chief David Hawk puts it, "she is an international tramp with an appetite for booze and drugs and not much else". Meow!

Pretty soon Carter's act of chivalry lands him in a pornographic blackmail plot turned into a grisly murder scene, complete with a mutilated corpse whose mouth is stuffed with its own genitals. Seizing the opportunity to put the pretty princess to work for Uncle Sam, Hawk sends Carter and her to Macao on a mission to trap Colonel Chun Li, head of Chinese Counter-Intelligence.

Did I mention that Chun Li has set out a trap to capture Carter in order to put his own nefarious scheme into motion?

By the time MACAO came out in 1968 the series most definitely out-Bonded James Bond to paraphrase a popular Killmaster series cover blurb of the day. Fleming was dead and any original Bond books from his pen were kaput. The film series had slowly but surely detoured away from the more espionage-oriented books into the somewhat cartoonish villainy of films like THUNDERBALL and YOU ONLY LIVE TWICE. Fans of Fleming's original novels could take solace in the world of the Killmaster complete with its super secret government agency and a gruff but fatherly boss who looked upon his deadliest agent as more than just a government assassin. (Other books in the series would further complete the bizarro Bond comparison thanks to a flirty secretary for Hawk and a Q-ish tech expert named Poindexter.)

If you've read even one of Fleming's 007 novels you'll probably find yourself enjoying MACAO much like I did – as a cut-rate Bond effort, right down to the hilarious description of a disguised Carter (whose cover image looks like a young Robert Wagner as pointed out by card-carrying Man of Action John Grace) pretending to be a nose-picking, cross-eyed coolie who shouts "No sabby. Want Hong Kong dolla now!" at a clerk he's just about to karate chop into submission. (I couldn't help but recall a giant, paunchy Sean Connery trying to pass for a Japanese fisherman in the unintentionally hilarious YOU ONLY LIVE TWICE.)

The storyline globe hops in typical Bond fashion, our hero and heroine find themselves chained naked in a basement dungeon awaiting a fate worse than death, the villain gladly shares his evil scheme with a chained Carter, and there's a shifty ally whom we're never quite sure we can trust.

Unlike the aforementioned SWAG and THE CHAMELEON, the KILLMASTER series would prove to be one of the most durable and long-running of the men's action series. DRAGON SLAY, the 261st (!) Nick Carter adventure was published in 1990... and you can be sure we'll have more to say about Carter in upcoming installments of BLOOD, BRAWLS & BULLETS. – *Dan Taylor*

THE BUTCHER #9: SEALED WITH BLOOD
by Stuart Johnson

The men's action explosion fueled by the success of The Executioner and The Destroyer meant that a lot of half-baked characters made their way onto the paperback racks. Though he lasted for 30+ novels (more than contemporary titles like The Protector and The Inquisitor), The Butcher definitely needed more time in the oven. And, perhaps, a bit more seasoning.

A former syndicate gunman skilled at planning and executing the Mob's nefarious schemes, Bucher (aka The Butcher) has quit the organization and lived. Despite protestations that "no one ever quits the organization and lives".

Now working as a planner/agent for the Feds, The Butcher decides to make one last check on a shipment of "farm implements" to Israel and finds himself getting surprised by a Mob gunman, which leads our hero to search for answers to questions, like "why is The Mob so interested in this shipment?", "how many people can I kill in and around this busy airport before I arouse suspicion?", and, "do I have adequate change for all the phone calls I'm going to make over the next 183 pages?".

After a series of deadly gun battles and explosions, The Butcher finds himself hoofing it to Israel where he teams with other government operatives to track down the "farm implements" that were whisked out of customs by enemy forces once they reached Israel.

Though I originally thought this installment was written by prolific tie-in and pulp vet Michael Avallone, it turns out my info was faulty and the real author is believed to be James Dockery. (Avallone would eventually come on board and bang out the last nine entries in the series according to the indispensible SpyGuysAndGals.com.) Filled with page upon page of stilted, stiff dialogue, this Butcher adventure is more like The Debater.

If you're interested in endless passages about whether or not an overhead door has a keyhole, phone calls and discussions about what the good guys should do in case the bad guys do A followed by additional plans in case the bad guys do B, then SEALED WITH BLOOD is for you.

I actually read this installment a year or so ago and

couldn't imagine it was as bad as I remembered. A quick reread – coupled with recent reads of better titles – proved that it's actually worse than I recalled. – Dan Taylor

NINJA MASTER #1: VENGEANCE IS HIS
by Wade Barker

If, as ER scribe John Grace once quipped, ARROW is like the most violent episode of THE YOUNG & THE RESTLESS ever produced, the debut of Brett Wallace aka Ninja Master is like the most violent Aaron Spelling pilot that never got a green light.

A sometimes sleazy, frequently violent entry in Warner's short-lived 'Men of Action' book series (see pages 24 and 27 for reviews of a couple Dirty Harry novels from the same line), NINJA MASTER is basically a pulpy updating of Batman/Bruce Wayne... with kung-fu.

Brett Ashford is the son of wealthy Ohio socialites (?!) and has just announced that he and his Japanese wife, Kyoko, are going to be parents. But when thrill-seeking bikers murder his parents and pregnant wife while he's off being a designated driver, Brett does what any right-thinking American would do and leaves the case in the hands of the justice system.

Unfortunately, an F. Lee Bailey-esque defense attorney gets the case against the bikers tossed on a technicality and Asford does what any super-rich dude with a martial arts background would do... he creates a super-rich alias, murders the bikers, beefs up his Ninja training in the Orient and sets out to be a righter of wrongs for America's downtrodden.

If THE BUTCHER #9 (see previous page) gets dinged for being too talky and hung up on exposition, NINJA MASTER #1 gets bonus points for having the same dramatic economy as James Glickenhaus' neo-Bolan flick THE EXTERMINATOR starring Robert Ginty.

There's precious little time wasted on flowery prose about martial arts training or the Way of the Ninja. Nope, Ashford/Wallace exacts revenge for the murders, heads to the Orient, spends nine years sharpening his skills and announces his plan to offer his services "to those who are terrorized, brutalized by others and have no one to turn to" – all in the space of 14 pages!

Once back on American shores Wallace romances a bosomy Japanese chef and cracks the skulls of some gang members who have been terrorizing an LA neighborhood inhabited by a hooker with a heart of gold (I'd have cast a Landers sister for the pilot), a bevy of elderly residents (shades of Cannon's 1985 DEATH WISH 3), and Sid, a Navy vet who drinks beer and lets his fists do the talking (James Arness?).

Wallace's final plan all plays out a little too quickly – even given the author's penchant for brevity – and for something called 'Ninja Master' there's precious little in the way of actual "Ninja" shenanigans. But the whole thing is a breezy, 189 pages that was better than I'd been led to believe.

Our own Men of Action suggest the series got better (and sleazier) as it progresses and I'm already itching to crack the cover on later installments. Ric Meyers would pen some books in the original 'Ninja Master' run then cranked out a couple four-book sagas entitled 'Year of the Ninja Master' and 'War of the Ninja Master'. – Dan Taylor

THE DESTROYER #2: DEATH CHECK
by Warren Murphy and Richard Sapir

One of the many joys of Warren Murphy and Richard Sapir's *Destroyer* series is the way the books combine no-nonsense prose and hard-boiled machismo with pulpy plotlines. The whole plot of DEATH CHECK is ludicrous and yet it's involving, fast-paced, and quite a fun read. And when you're dabbling in such pulpy excess, it is important to hook your audience at the very start. And boy is the opening of DEATH CHECK real grabber: An unsuspecting Average Joe gets shot up with a lethal dose of heroin by a killer while a topless dominatrix brandishing a whip looks on. And if that doesn't get your attention I don't know what will.

Remo Williams is assigned by CURE head honcho Harold Smith to solve the mysterious death. He takes over the dead man's position as security advisor to a top secret government think tank, does some snooping and pretty soon learns of a plot to take over the world using mind control.

World domination by mind control is a familiar gimmick in pulp novels, and it's trotted out yet again here. But the authors find subtle tweaks on the formula that made this reader smirk and smile more than a few times. I mean, would it surprise you to learn that the villain behind the plot is a chess-obsessed Nazi? Of course not. But even when using the simplest most basic ingredients, a great chef can bake one heck of a cake. And that is what makes readers come back time and again to the *Destroyer* novels: It may be junk food, but boy does it ever hit

THE MANY FACES OF REMO AND CHIUN, MASTER OF SINANJU

the spot.

Murphy and Sapir are an efficient, economical writing team and DEATH CHECK features several spellbinding passages. I really loved the way Remo is described sneaking around a darkened gym: "He breathed deeply, and slid through the dark, in almost imperceptible movements... He wore black tennis shoes... [and] a tee shirt dyed black. His shorts were black. Night moving in night."

And they sure know how to write action. My favorite bit comes early in the book when Remo encounters some thugs in a paint store and he breaks their spines, crushes their testicles, and decapitates one guy by sticking his head into a paint-mixing machine. He also beats up a bunch of bikers and has a battle-for-a-parachute scene worthy of James Bond, too.

All in all, this is definitely one check worth picking up. – Mitch Lovell

THE DESTROYER #21: DEADLY SEEDS
by Warren Murphy and Richard Sapir

A greedy industrialist named Fielding finds out he only has 18 months to live. He then sets out on a grand scheme to drive the world into famine and cooks up a phony scam involving a miracle foodstuff called "Wondergrain" that he claims can be grown anywhere in the world. Remo and Chiun catch on to Fielding's plan and set out to stop him.

The villain's plot is more complicated than it really needed to be. There is a lot of rigmarole involving Fielding's meddling with the stock market that wastes a lot of time, and in addition to a terminally ill megalomaniacal villain, Murphy and Sapir also manage to toss in some mobsters and ninjas as peripheral bad guys. Not that I'm not the kind of guy to complain about adding ninjas to anything, but it does overcrowd the plot.

But that's okay because whenever Remo and Chiun are front and center, DEADLY SEEDS is quite a lot of fun. The banter between the two is priceless with one especially funny passage featuring attempting to make Chiun an equal partner in a potential enterprise; but, my favorite moments in the book involve Chiun getting all worked up over his afternoon soap operas. And, of course, Remo's constant needling of his superior, Dr. Harold Smith is pretty funny, too.

The action is solid for the most part, especially since Remo is fighting everyone from overzealous bodyguards to Mafioso to Ninjas and he has plenty of fodder to work with. The highlight, though, features Chiun being challenged to a game of pool by some thugs.

And while the plot meanders a bit, Murphy and Sapir's prose is crisp. There were several instances where just the simplest phrases cracked me up. My favorite passage: "He was in his late forties and his face was a remnant of a teenage battle with acne. The acne had won." – Mitch Lovell

THE DESTROYER #25: SWEET DREAMS
by Warren Murphy and Ric Meyers

Dr. William Westhead Wooley has invented "The Dreamocizer", a device that promises to revolutionize the entertainment industry – and put television and movies out of business at the same time. With the attachment of a few simple electrodes, users can watch their

most secret fantasies played out on their TV set.

In full color.

With stereophonic sound an optional extra.

The mob wants to push it as the ultimate vice, the television networks want to bury it so bad they send buxom network star Patti Shea to seduce Wooley (or kill him), and Dr. Harold Smith of CURE sees the device's potential as a tool for law enforcement, mental health institutions and prisons.

Naturally, all these forces – plus Remo Williams and Chiun – collide on the campus of Edgewood University in St. Louis as Wooley sets about meeting with bidders interested in "acquiring" The Dreamocizer.

Remo – who is tiring of being "perfect" and wants to be happy – seems far less interested in any of the device's commercial or sociological applications and simply wants a house. Which is why The Destroyer agrees to meet Smith in St. Louis to get to the bottom of The Dreamocizer and the mob's interest.

Aside from DESTROYER #14: JUDGMENT DAY I'm more used to Smith occupying his office at Folcroft Sanitarium; so having him accompany Remo and Chiun on a mission feels a bit extraneous, though it does lead to some hysterical passages where an obsessed Remo presses the CURE head on the house he dreams about. Perhaps, because this is the first Destroyer novel featuring a writer other than series creators Warren Murphy and Richard Sapir, it was inevitable that the book would shake up the series' usual structure.

Though there are moments in the book that echo previous installments I'd read – I tend to juxtapose the darts scene in SWEET DREAMS with the pool scene in DEADLY SEEDS – Murphy and Myers do a first-rate job of juggling the series' backstory, the Remo/Chiun interaction and even some violence that seems jarring even for a Destroyer novel.

Best of all, though, is the book's final few pages in which Remo and Chiun discuss home and dreams, their father/son partnership expressed in such a touching fashion that it made this old softie want to tear up. – *Dan Taylor*

THE DESTROYER #31: THE HEAD MEN
by Warren Murphy and Richard Sapir

The President has become a target for assassination. He thinks he has plenty of security around him and foolishly puts his faith in the Secret Service. For his own good, Smith must prove the President wrong. So he sends Remo and Chiun to infiltrate the White House to show the President that he isn't completely untouchable.

The tongue-in-cheek set-up for THE HEAD MEN had me laughing out loud. And the part where Remo sneaks into the White House undetected and introduces himself to the President in the White House bathroom is a classic.

The banter between Remo and Chiun is also first rate and I especially liked when Smith puts Chiun in charge, which of course means he really puts the verbal screws to Remo. Even the repartee between Remo and Smith is quite funny:

> "So the President is going to be killed. So what?" Remo said.
>
> "Have you seen the Vice President?" Smith said.
>
> "We must save the President," Remo said.

The villain in this one is somewhat over the top. The wheelchair-bound "crippled dwarf" (as Remo calls him) goes around threatening the President, ogling women, and giving people mind-control cocktails. Of course, once he goes head-to-head with Remo it's no contest, but I liked the lengths Murphy and Sapir went through to make him despicable.

Some of this gets a bit TOO ludicrous. The scene where Remo "hails a cab" is kinda silly, but hey, it's still enjoyable. Remo also has a run-in with some decidedly un-PC fake Arabs that's funny.

The writing, overall, is pretty crisp. Some of the chapters involving the President dealing with assassination threats and blackmail tend to drag, but the finale is a lot of fun and the dialogue is rather terrific. My favorite Remo line: "You're as loose as lambshit!" – *Mitch Lovell*

Available Now! It's THE BEST (AND WORST) OF THE VIDEO VACUUM by Mitch Lovell

Watch Mitch as he draws his crosshairs on the Twilight Saga! Journey with him as he delves into the world of The Great White Ninjas! Marvel as he sits through several awful sequels and emerges with his sanity (mostly) intact! From low budget stinkers, to the latest Hollywood blockbusters, it's all filtered through Mitch's unique (some would say, demented) viewpoint. Paperback and Kindle Versions available at Amazon.com.

"I loved this so much!" – Robin Bougie, CINEMA SEWER/GRAPHIC THRILLS

THE DESTROYER: THE

I love to read series novels – to see the continuing development of characters and their further adventures. In fact, nothing irks me more than to get a great book, really like the characters and then that's it. Nothing about them ever again. The Author wants me to move on.

But I can't. I'm a monogamist reader. I form strong attachments to characters and worlds I like.

I blame Jack London for this. The first novel I ever read was *Call of the Wild*. I was in the third grade. I then went back and read *White Fang*. I loved them. And I was hooked on the idea that characters can leap from the pages of one book and land comfortably in the next.

I've read a lot of great series over the years. Edgar Rice Burroughs' *Tarzan* series was fantastic. From there I moved on to C.S. Forrester's *Horatio Hornblower*, Robert E. Howard's *Conan*, and Lester Dent's *Doc Savage*. But there has always been one series for me that is head and shoulders above the rest.

The Destroyer.

I was first exposed to Remo Williams when I was in high school. My best friend's dad had been reading Remo's adventures for many years. My pal had read a few but wasn't as keen on the series as his dad. But he was sure that if I liked reading series, I'd love Remo. He insisted the action and satire were right up my alley.

He knew me very well.

What's not to like about The Destroyer? It's got ass-whoopery galore, cutting satire, dry humor, chicks, spy stuff and even the occassional explosion – or boom, as Master Chiun would call it.

Remo Williams starts out as an everyman. A simple beat cop framed for a murder he didn't commit. But after his supposed execution, instead of waking up at the Pearly Gates, he wakes up in the clutches of a secret organization that is out to save America from itself.

As a young man dreaming of a career in the military, and an avid student of Tae Kwon Do, the series had me hooked with book #1 (*Created: The Destroyer*) which I was lucky enough to read first. I read a grocery bag of them that first year, in order, but not a complete run.

I read as Remo Williams was trained in the ancient art of Sinanju – the sun source of martial arts, and the means by which the House of Sinanju had been dispatching ne'erdowells for thousands of years. I read how Remo developed a father-son relationship with his instructor – the inscrutable Korean Master Chiun (who had a sharp wit and dry sense of humor that often reminded me of Bud Abbott or Jack Benny).

I eventually dropped out of my own martial arts studies. And my military plans greatly changed, with my dreams of being a parachuting green beret altered to a USAF cop for only a short four years. But I kept reading. For years.

Sun Source of Series

And that is why The Destroyer is the king in my book. 150 novels over the past forty years. That's ten times the adventures Tarzan ever had. It might even be more than Doc Savage.

150 adventures that all were written with the same basic formula, but each of which always seemed like something new. Forget comic books. I was always waiting for the next Destroyer novel.

The only thing that stopped my reading was becoming a father. The books became harder to get as I got older, and when I had a wife and daughter to spend most of my time with it became harder to get to the bookstore before the few copies they carried of the latest relief flew off the shelves.

And I apparently cleared out the used bookstores in my area in my quest to get a full collection. Not that it was ever easy to find the old books. Most Destroyer fans seem to only part with their beloved tomes upon death.

Now it's 2014, and The Destroyer is back. Which is odd timing for me – for years, I wanted to write as well. Inspired by the awesomeness of The Destroyer. But without Sinanju training, I was never able to push past the depths of the slush piles, and my feeble attempts remained lost in obscurity. That changed when I discovered self-publishing in 2012. I launched my own series, hoping to blend what I liked about Tarzan, Doc Savage, and The Destroyer into one series. And in the process of trying to promote my work, I learned the Destroyer was back with new adventures!

Even better, all those paperbacks I missed over the years, or the ones I never could find to complete my collection... they're all coming out in electronic format! I'll soon be able to read the ENTIRE series! In order!

It just doesn't get any better than that.

The Destroyer has got a lot of steam left in him. He's even spun off a new series, *Legacy*, by series creator Warren Murphy and Gerald Welch – a fan of the series-turned writer. It tells the tale of Remo Williams' son and daughter, as they receive Sinanju training and join the battle to protect America on a totally different front from Remo.

So now it's just a matter of time – sitting back and waiting for the next Sinanju adventure to come out. My kids are old enough now that I actually get the time to read here and there. And my first choice for reading is always going to be Sinanju. – *C.E. Martin*

C.E. Martin is a USAF veteran and a criminal investigator with over 20 years combined experience in the civilian and military criminal justice systems. C.E. lives and writes in Southern Indiana with his wife and children. When asked for his favorite Destroyer book he replied that he is partial to #100. For more on C.E. and his books visit stonesoldiersbooks.blogspot.com.

ER #52 :: page 34

REMO WILLIAMS:
The Adventure Begins (& Ends?)

REMO WILLIAMS: THE ADVENTURE BEGINS (aka REMO: THE FIRST ADVENTURE, REMO: UNARMED AND DANGEROUS) (1985)

REMO WILLIAMS: THE ADVENTURE BEGINS stands as one of the great missed opportunities in cinema history. In a perfect world, we would've had at least a dozen Remo Williams movies by now. However, the film didn't exactly set the box office on fire, so producer Dick Clark didn't feel it necessary to create a franchise around Remo. But you can tell he really WANTED to. The fact that Clark hired Guy (GOLDFINGER) Hamilton to direct the flick and Christopher (MOONRAKER) Wood to write the script makes you think he was hoping to create a franchise to rival the Bond series. Alas, it just wasn't meant to be. (There was also a failed TV pilot/sequel that unsuccessfully tried to launch the character.)

And it's a shame, too, because if there ever was a literary property to make movie series around, it's Richard Sapir and Warren Murphy's *Destroyer* novels. With over a hundred novels in the series, there is certainly a wealth of material to choose from. As expected, the film follows the basic outline of the first Destroyer book. *(Ed. Note: In an interview in THE ASSASSIN'S HANDBOOK Murphy & Sapir suggest a take on a script for the flick went in an entirely different direction than the big screen adaptation and a script from the pair written in the 1970s is available as a download from Amazon.)*

As in the books the secret government organization CURE (whose motto is "Thou shalt not get away with it.") specializes in executing criminals who are above the law. CURE recruits a tough cop (Fred Ward) to be their assassin, and after a round of plastic surgery, they christen him "Remo Williams". (Making him the world's first hero named after a bedpan.) The Korean "Master of Sinanju", Chiun (Joel Grey), trains Remo for his first mission, and the two form a bond that is the core of the movie.

REMO WILLIAMS: THE ADVENTURE BEGINS gets the heart of the novels right. The interaction between Remo and Chiun is about as great as you could hope for with Ward and Grey perfectly cast. Their chemistry is undeniable and scenes of the two bickering make you wish this had been a blockbuster that led to a series.

The biggest debit of the film: The villain is awfully lame. George Coe never quite seems menacing enough, and his scheme (selling faulty weapons) probably wouldn't have cut the mustard on an episode of THE A-TEAM. (Coe's henchmen, Michael Pataki and Patrick Kilpatrick fare much better though.) And the future Captain Janeway, Kate Mulgrew makes for a weak leading lady, although admittedly she really wasn't given much to work with.

Hamilton's direction is a bit flat, but he pulls off some solid action sequences. The scenes of Remo and Chiun dodging bullets obviously inspired THE MATRIX. (And they work better here since they're not a lot of flashy special effects involved.) Remo's run-in with some super-smart guard dogs is hilarious, which is a good showcase for Hamilton's knack for combining action and comedy. The highlight of course, is the scene where Remo fights some goons on the scaffolding of the Statue of Liberty while it's under renovation. It's simply one of the best-staged action scenes of the 80s.

The thing that knocks the flick down a notch is the pacing, which is odd since most of the books are paced like lightning. The film, however, suffers from much of the same bloat that takes the wind of out many a Bond film. But despite its flaws, REMO WILLIAMS: THE ADVENTURE BEGINS is still quite a lot of fun. – Mitch Lovell

As we readied this issue for press came some big news... not only was a big screen trilogy based on the Mack Bolan Executioner novels being prepped but Sony had tapped Destroyer fan Shane Black (IRON MAN 3) to helm Remo and Chiun's return to the multiplex! Though there was no news on casting as of press date, fans were encouraged by Black's attachment as well as news that Destroyer author James Mullaney was involved with the script.

Foot to the Face Cinema

MEMORIAL DAY (1998/Artisan)

An uncredited Joe Estevez laments the end of the Cold War. Defense spending is down. There are no more villains left for America to fight. His plan to revitalize the military: create a fictional terrorist cell code-named "Red Five" to be a viable threat to the United States. Using a satellite missile system, "Red Five" targets and destroys several military installations. The idea is that once Congress thinks our nation is under attack, they'll OK more military spending. I mean who cares that thousands of our own people are dying? Just as long as Joe Estevez gets to generate a little income for his covert ops, right?

Anyway, Joe's masterstroke is to set up "The Perfect Weapon" himself, Jeff Speakman, as the patsy. You see, Jeff used to be a great soldier, but became a thorn in Joe's side when he blew the whistle on one of Joe's schemes. He threw Jeff in the nuthouse for that little stunt for several years, and he was given so many shock treatments that he doesn't know whether he's coming or going. Joe pulls Jeff out of the asylum and gives him the assignment to whack a politician (who's essentially Joe's puppet). But just as Jeff is about to pull the trigger, he remembers his past and goes on the lam. With the help of a feisty reporter (hey, aren't they all "feisty" in these movies?) he sets out to put an end to the "Red Five" conspiracy.

That plot description may seem pretty dense, but the film isn't hard to follow at all. Despite all of the shadowy cloak and dagger developments, the first half of the film moves along briskly. Believe or not, I found myself rather enthralled by the early scenes. I have to hand it to the filmmakers – the idea of the military creating a fictional villain to attack our own soil to justify its own existence is pretty ingenious. Too bad the great set-up gives way to a lukewarm action flick.

If you go into MEMORIAL DAY on the basis of seeing Jeff Speakman kick some ass, you're bound to be disappointed. Sad to say, he spends most of the first half of the film strapped to a hospital gurney. And once he finally shakes off his brainwashing and goes into Hero Mode he isn't given that many opportunities to strut his stuff. If you've seen THE PERFECT WEAPON or STREET KNIGHT you know Speakman has the (karate) chops to carry a movie. However, in MEMORIAL DAY, his use of Kenpo karate is limited to only a handful of scenes.

Director Worth Keeter, writer Steve Latshaw and producer Andrew Stevens were also responsible for the Speakman flick SCORPIO ONE. Both films share the same space shuttle footage (which is repeated over and over again), and there's a brief action scene from that film that's used here as a flashback. And speaking of footage from other movies, the submarine scenes were swiped from THE HUNT FOR RED OCTOBER. – Mitch Lovell

RED SCORPION aka RED EXTERMINATOR (1989/Synapse)

After attaining stardom playing Ivan Drago in ROCKY IV, Dolph Lundgren went on to star as He-Man in MASTERS OF THE UNIVERSE. But it wasn't until 1989's RED SCORPION that Dolph got to flex his muscles in a straight-up action movie. It was a step up from the silly MASTERS OF THE UNIVERSE flick, but RED SCORPION proved that – at least at this point in his career – Lundgren was only about as good as the material he was given. (That would soon change with his next picture, THE PUNISHER.)

Nikolai (Lundgren) is Russia's top solider. He's given an assignment to gain a revolutionary's trust before assassinating him. Predictably, Nikolai refuses to carry out his orders and is tortured by his superiors. He is somehow able to escape his captors and flees to the desert where he is nursed back to health by a mystical shaman. Nikolai has an epiphany and decides to take up arms against his former comrades.

I'm a big Dolph Lundgren fan, but even I admit this isn't his finest hour. There are some scenes where you can obviously tell he was still learning his craft. In the pivotal scene where he has his big change of heart and decides to fight against his county it should be a big rallying moment. But since he just has a blank stare on his face the whole time it's hard to really tell what he's feeling. He did a great job physically with the role (his character is more or less

Rambo by way of Ivan Drago), but he just didn't have the acting chops at this point to fully pull off the character's transformation.

INVASION USA's Joseph Zito directed and does a competent job behind the camera. He handles the explosions and gunfire well and there is some memorable gore and deaths by machete thrown in for good measure. (I guess Zito was still trying to remind everyone he directed FRIDAY THE 13TH PART 4.) So, just for the action alone, RED SCORPION is hard to completely dismiss.

Zito does allow the pacing to slow to a crawl during the dull scenes between Dolph and the medicine man. I'm not saying they're as bad as the medicine man scenes from Steven Seagal's ON DEADLY GROUND, but they're pretty rough. Zito never quite gets the film's momentum back on track after that, despite the decent finale. Another debit is the film's bloated 105-minute running time. (The Synapse disc presents the original, uncut version of the film.)

Overall, I can't quite recommend RED SCORPION, but it is an important stepping stone in Dolph Lundgren's career. But if you're a big Dolph fan like, you'll probably want to check out Synapse's Blu Ray release of the film as they really went all out with the extras. The crown jewel is the documentary HELL HATH NO FURY: DOLPH LUNDGREN AND THE ROAD TO RED SCORPION, a 24-minute interview with Dolph produced by Ballyhoo Motion Pictures. It's a very candid interview and he talks a lot about the early days of his career, which is really interesting. Dolph discusses everything from dating Grace Jones and getting picked on the fly to play a henchman in A VIEW TO A KILL, to the problems of playing a live-action toy (and wearing a loincloth), to the tumultuous shooting schedule of RED SCORPION. It's an enormously entertaining interview that easily outshines the main feature.

We also get ASSIGNMENT: AFRICA, a 13-minute interview with producer Jack Abramoff, produced by Red Shirt Pictures. Abramoff offers up some informative behind-the-scenes information, but he's just not the storyteller Dolph is. Red Shirt Pictures also was responsible for SCORPION TALES, a 9-minute interview with Tom Savini, who did the make-up effects for the film. He talks about his impromptu hiring and the challenges of creating the effects with a limited schedule. We're also privy to some of Savini's personal photos and home movies from the set, also presented on the disc in unedited form. There's also the usual poster and still gallery, theatrical trailer, and a bunch of TV spots too.

Rounding out the extras is the feature length audio commentary by director Joseph Zito, moderated by Nathaniel Thompson. It's an easy listen and there are virtually no lulls in the discussion. Surprisingly, of all the anecdotes Zito tells, the stories revolving around MISSING IN ACTION are the most interesting. (Sadly, they don't go into all the details.) – *Mitch Lovell*

THE SOLDIER aka CODE NAME: THE SOLDIER (1982/MGM)

Director James Glickenhaus' follow-up to the cult classic THE EXTERMINATOR is a crackling good Cold War thriller. The Russians are planning to detonate a plutonium bomb in an oil field in the Middle East, effectively irradiating half of the world's oil supply. It's up to The Soldier (WISEGUY's Ken Wahl) and his team to protect America's interests and stop the bomb from going off.

THE SOLDIER feels like a paperback potboiler brought to life. The plot is fairly preposterous, but is played deadly seriously, which ups to stakes considerably. There are only the briefest moments of levity (most come courtesy of Wahl's right-hand man, Steve James) and Glickenhaus sells the urgency of the situation wonderfully. The excellent globe-hopping location work (Berlin, St. Anton, New York, etc.) also lends authenticity to the action and the moody Tangerine Dream score is a perfect complement to Glickenhaus' style.

Glickenhaus also does a great job in the action department and delivers several memorable sequences. There is a great bar fight in a honkytonk saloon (while a young George Strait performs) that is a fine showcase for Steve James' kung fu skills. We also get an awesome car stunt in which Wahl jumps a Porsche over the Berlin Wall. (I guess you could say this movie has Wahl to Wall action?) There's also a terrific ski slope shootout that's as good as anything in a Bond movie. And while the film is not nearly as dark or as trashy as Glickenhaus' THE EXTERMINATOR, there is one memorably nasty bit in which an enemy agent turns a light bulb into deadly weapon.

The cast is uniformly solid. Ken Wahl is quite good. His screen presence exists somewhere in the middle ground between Richard Gere and Sylvester Stallone. He's got the all-American pretty boy looks, but there is a quiet toughness about him that makes him an ideal leading man. Steve James shines as his karate-chopping second in command. And Klaus Kinski has a brief but memorable role as a backstabbing double agent.

In short, action fans should salute THE SOLDIER. – Mitch Lovell

STRIKE COMMANDO 2 aka HEROIN FORCE (1988/Avid)

The original STRIKE COMMANDO was one of those lightning-in-a-bottle kinds of movies. I think the term "So Bad It's Good" is overused, but it certainly fit the bill when describing STRIKE COMMANDO. Written by TROLL 2's Claudio Fragasso and directed by NIGHT OF THE ZOMBIES' Bruno Mattei, STRIKE COMMANDO had the kind of behind-the-camera talent that was going to make it awesome. But the icing on the cake was the insane leading performance by Reb Brown as John Ransom.

Sadly, Brown did not return for STRIKE COMMANDO 2. Brent Huff takes over the role of Ransom, but it just isn't the same. Let's face it, no one can say, "Move! Move! Move! Go! Go! Go!" like Reb. Huff does try though, God bless him. Although he cranks the volume on his voice up to 11 during the action scenes, it winds up just seeming like a hollow imitation of Brown. Lucky for us, Fragasso and Mattei were once again on board for the second installment, so thank God for small favors.

The lightning maybe different, but at least we've got the same bottle.

Vic Jenkins (Richard Harris) saved Ransom's life in Vietnam. Ransom long believed Jenkins died in combat, but once he learns he's alive and under CIA custody, Ransom tracks him down. Of course, the villains trail Ransom and kidnap Jenkins. They demand $10 million in diamonds, but Ransom being Ransom, opts to rescue him instead.

I'm a sucker for a good Made-in-the-Philippines action movie, especially if it's got Vic Diaz in it. STRIKE COMMANDO 2 isn't good; but it was made in the Philippines, has a lot of action, and features Vic Diaz. Okay, so maybe I'm just a sucker.

Say what you will about the movie, but it does have Diaz playing a perverted prison guard, which instantly gives it an edge over any film that *doesn't* have Vic Diaz playing a perverted prison guard.

It's also fun seeing Richard Harris in this. Most distinguished actors starring in Italian productions shot in the Philippines have a habit of phoning it in. Harris, however, resists the temptation and delivers a solid performance. This, of course, makes him stick out like a sore thumb in such schlocky surroundings, but that's part of the charm.

STRIKE COMMANDO 2 hits the notes you'd expect from the RAMBO rip-off subgenre. There's a scene where our hero is tortured and electrocuted. There's also a part where he shoots up an empty room with a machine gun while screaming the villain's name in slow motion. And naturally, a lot of bamboo huts blow up during the finale.

But STRIKE COMMANDO 2 has my respect because of the way it also manages to rip-off RAIDERS OF THE LOST ARK. Mattei gives us a variation of the drinking game scene and even goes so far as to recreate the famous bar fight. The only difference is that the villain uses Ninjas for hired muscle. Later, there is a reprise of the RAIDERS motif as we get a riff on the classic truck chase, again with Ninjas subbing for the Nazis.

I'm sure you're reading this and saying to yourself, "Vic Diaz... Ninjas... what's not to like?" Well, the movie does have its fair share of highlights. Just know that the gaps in between the highlights are considerable.

I had problems with the fact that Ransom gets saddled with an annoying love interest. Well, she isn't exactly a love interest because she shoots up a bunch of stuff, too. You don't normally see that kind of behavior from a love interest in movies. But while her actions may be novel, she does have a tendency to grate on your nerves. I mean Huff isn't the best leading man, but he could've carried the movie all by himself without her tagging along.

And if you're a fan of the original, you can't help but be disappointed by this flick. Remember how great the final fight was in that movie? Well, the climactic brawl in this one suffers in comparison. There are some nutty moments here to be sure. My favorite was the scene where Ransom goes overboard while subduing a guard. (He hits him about six times more than necessary.) It would've looked at home in A FISTFUL OF YEN.

Overall, STRIKE COMMANDO 2 has its moments. That's about all it has, but those moments are definitely keepers. However, the flick just lacks the jaw-dropping insanity that made the original film a classic. – *Mitch Lovell*

SEXY KILLER aka THE DRUG CONNECTION (1976/Intercontinental Video)

Two years earlier the U.S. film TNT JACKSON (1974, reviewed on page 41) failed miserably at combining the black exploitation and Hong Kong martial arts genres. It starred Jeanne Bell, a poor man's Pam Grier, who goes on a personal vendetta against a Chinese drug ring. This train wreck of a film managed to get just about everything wrong.

By contrast, Hong Kong's SEXY KILLER approaches the same genre blend from a different angle and succeeds brilliantly. This fast-paced crime yarn is directly inspired by COFFY (1973), Pam Grier's biggest Blaxploitation hit, with Grier playing a nurse turned vigilante who takes revenge on the drug dealers who hooked her little sister on heroin.

Beguiling beauty Chen Ping, the queen of '70s Hong Kong exploitation movies, plays nurse Gao Wan Fei, the Pam Grier role. The plots are more or less the same as Gao seeks revenge against the gangsters that raped and drugged up her sister.

Chen was one of the few HK film actresses who did both erotic and action roles, and this version outdoes the Grier flick in sex, violence, and overall sleaze. Gao works her way up the crime syndicate hierarchy by seducing and killing several drug dealers. Her weapon of choice is a nifty double-bladed knife concealed in a metal bracelet. In a memorable early scene (shot in slow-motion), a topless Gao engages in a brutal fight to the death with a pusher.

Yueh Hua plays a hot-headed cop assigned to the case and also serves as an eventual love interest. Subplots about corrupt cops, a shady politician, numerous kung fu melees, murders, a cat-fight, and frequent nudity keep the story moving along at a brisk pace. The film makes good use of ugly industrial sites and half-constructed buildings for its fight scenes and mob killings. There is also a surprising amount of effective on-the-run filming with hand-held cameras during the action sequences.

Like most crime drama/action films, the characters are thinly painted with little depth or nuance. The most (potentially) interesting character is the depraved big boss drug lord (played by an over-the-top Wang Hsia). His house has a fully-equipped S&M sex dungeon and he gets in the mood by watching 8mm porno films while whipping his mistress/sex slave.

Without giving too much away, suffice to say the explosive climax involves crashing a car into the kingpin's house and blasting everyone to hell with a shotgun. But how a registered nurse got to be so skilled with firearms and ass-kicking martial arts is anyone's guess.

This was followed by the popular sequel, LADY EXTERMINATOR (1977), with most of the same cast and director. — *Jim Ivers*

THE PACKAGE (2012/Anchor Bay)

Oh Hollywood. Why do you work so hard at trying to convince me the next generation of action stars is made up of guys like Justin Timberlake, Ryan Phillipe and Taylor Lautner? Couldn't you have spent – I don't know? – a third of the budget from something like ABDUCTION on developing projects for an action star with real screen presence? A guy I'd actually believe has been in a fight over something more than the last crepe at the craft services table? A guy like the actor formerly known as Stone Cold Steve Austin?

When action cinema blew up in the late 80s thanks to hits like DIE HARD, ABOVE THE LAW and BLOODSPORT everybody had their favorite stars. At the time I was definitely a Seagal guy, enjoyed a sprinkling of Van Damme (a little too much focus on the butt cheeks for me to go all in on JCVD) and had a serious action jones for the sorta-straight-to-VHS adventures of Wings Hauser (DEAD MAN WALKING, NO SAFE HAVEN, LA BOUNTY).

But these days, nothing freezes me in my tracks like

the bald pate and sinister stare – equally at home on his good and bad guys – of Steve Austin. Stumble upon one of his adventures while trawling Netflix? Added to the queue! Catch a glimpse of him glowering at me from the Redbox poster? Reserved! And, I have to say, I haven't been let down yet. Sure, he seems ill at ease delivering quips as he offs baddies in HUNT TO KILL (2010) but it's a fun recreation of a long-in-the-tooth genre. Okay, I'll admit he and Seagal might have zero chemistry in MAXIMUM CONVICTION (2012) but you can't take your eyes off the hulking, creaky wrestler as he dispatches bad guys and tosses out lines like "Alright, which one of you motherfuckers killed my future ex-wife?!".

So I was particularly pleased when I saw him splitting the cover of THE PACKAGE with Dolph Lundgren, another reliable, go-to star of the direct-to-video action set. (I'm also a sucker for anything with Brit martial artist Scott Adkins, though I get the feeling he's one break from larger things.)

Directed by Jesse Johnson – the stuntman-turned-director whose faux 'Wonder Woman' trailer generated a ton of buzz – and written by Derek Kolstad, THE PACKAGE feels like what would result if Larry Cohen and Quentin Tarantino got together to make a direct-to-video actioner.

Austin stars as Tommy, a mid-level collector who accepts an unusual, but worthwhile, job from his boss, Big Doug (Eric Keenleyside): deliver a mysterious package to The German (Lundgren) and the debt owed to Doug by Tommy's loser brother will be wiped clean. Eager to help his brother and, perhaps, start a new life with his galpal, Tommy sets off on his route, unaware that he's now the target of every lowlife and enforcer between him and The German.

It's not long before he runs afoul of a team of soldiers-turned-mercs led by Devon (Darren Shahlavi) as well as Anthony (Michael Dangierfield), a rival mobster who sends his sidekick (90s action star Jerry Trimble) to intercept Tommy and "the package".

Johnson's lengthy background as a stuntman is on full display as THE PACKAGE crackles with gun battles and close quarter fights, including a knock-down construction site tilt between Trimble and Austin that had me itching to go back and reacquaint myself with Trimble's full slate of 90s action efforts like ONE MAN ARMY (1994), LIVE BY THE FIST (1993) and BREATHING FIRE (1991... with Bolo!).

Though Austin is certainly the star it's nice to see Lundgren get to flex his fighting and acting muscles as the nattily-attired villain, The German. Despite being glaringly doubled in some of the fight sequences, Lundgren can still trade punches with the best of them and a scene where he schools an off-screen foe about the benefits of eating healthy had me dying. There's something to be said for an action "hero" who can look past billing and audience expectations in order to take a bite out of a meaty, supporting role.

So come on, Hollywood. If THE EXPENDABLES flicks and the (relative) success of Jason Statham have taught us anything it's that audiences still want to see real men in their action cinema. Do us all a favor a ditch the pretty boys. – Dan Taylor

COMMAND PERFORMANCE (2009/First Look)

Dolph Lundgren has been getting his share of ink lately thanks to roles in Stallone's EXPENDABLES flicks, not to mention John Hyams' fun reanimation of the long-thought-mothballed UNIVERSAL SOLDIER series. But you'd be wise to keep your eyes peeled when walking through the local dollar store or steering around the bargain DVD bin at your local supermarket, because the Dolph-helmed COMMAND PERFORMANCE might be the best of the bunch.

Like the thousands of DIE HARD-inspired actioners that have come before it, COMMAND's set-up is as simple as it gets: Joe (Lundgren) is the drummer for a Russian rock band on the brink of success, but things go horribly wrong when Soviet extremists take over a concert by Venus (Melissa Molinaro), an American pop sensation performing for the widowed Russian President (Hristo Shopov) and his adolescent daughters. Teaming up with the President's new head of security, Joe must employ the skills learned in his shadowy past to take out the bad guys and save the day.

Dismissed early in his career as lunkhead beefcake, Lundgren has been a steady, reliable presence in the action film marketplace over the years. Which is more than I can say about some of his 80s/90s action flick brethren. (Yeah, Big Steve, I'm looking at you.)

Despite a handful of well-known titles (MASTERS OF THE UNIVERSE, THE PUNISHER, RED SCORPION, SHOWDOWN IN LITTLE TOKYO), the bulk of Dolph's work has been fodder for the Redboxes, Netflixes and IMPACT channels of the world. And – seemingly interchangeable names aside – Lundgren's flicks are almost always more reliable than, say, some of the more "expandable" action stars of yesteryear. (Yes, Big Steve. Looking. Again.)

Plus, he seems less dickey than say Stallone, Snipes, JCVD or Seagal.

COMMAND also illustrates that Dolph has been doing more than chasing skirts and scarfing donuts on all these sets over the years. The flick feels far bigger than its presence as a dollar-bin castoff would suggest; there are big concert and crowd scenes, at least one explosive action sequence that blew me off my couch, convincing location settings and the overall sense that the action really is taking place in the bowels of a huge arena, not two hallways and a janitor's closet like the excruciating Seagal-versus-vampires actioner AGAINST THE DARK.

But the action – and the flick – is carried by Lundgren as Joe, the happy-go-lucky, pot-smoking, slightly mysterious drummer for CMF (which stands for Cheap Motherfucker in "honor" of their manager). The screenplay – credited to Lundgren and action stalwart Steve Latshaw – wisely avoids the easy out of having Joe be a member of some shadowy government force or cop whose wife and kids were blowed up real good by some filthy mobsters. Instead he's a little bit darker than your usual "fish out of water" action hero, which fits both the character and Lundgren's laid back, muscle-bound persona.

In a world where direct-to-video sequels are all the rage I have to admit I'm a little disappointed there's not an entire series of Joe The Drummer flicks. I would totally "rock and load" every single one of them. – *Dan Taylor*

TNT JACKSON (1974/Shout Factory)

This bargain basement attempt at blending black exploitation (Blaxploitation) with the chop-socky martial arts genre comes from Roger Corman's New World Pictures. The not-so-literate script was co-written by actor Dick Miller, a frequent player in Corman's films. Director Cirio H. Santiago worked, uncredited, on many Corman projects, three of which starred Pam Grier. As the titular ass-kicker Diana Jackson, shapely Jeannie Bell (Playboy's Playmate of the Month, October 1969) is one of several Grier lookalikes Santiago cast in his films.

The immense popularity of Bruce Lee/Kung Fu films pouring out of Hong Kong in the early '70s led to some inevitable, if unlikely, genre hybrids such as Hammer's THE LEGEND OF THE 7 GOLDEN VAMPIRES, also released in 1974. In a move that could be called "Foxy Brown Goes to Hong Kong", the casting of two black leads (Bell and Stan Shaw) gives TNT JACKSON the appearance of an urban Blaxpoitation film that's been uprooted and shoe-horned into an Oriental setting. The result is an awkward, implausible, fish-out-of-water feeling that never comes together.

The derivative revenge plot unfolds with Diana "TNT" Jackson, a foxy, karate-kicking babe, roaming the mean streets of Hong Kong after her brother is killed in a drug deal. Before you know it, everybody is Kung-Fu fighting – but these cats are not "fast as lightning". In fact, this has some of the slowest and least convincing martial arts scenes ever filmed. The fights look more like rehearsal footage as Bell tends to shove rather than hit her opponents. Even with these questionable skills she routinely pummels half a dozen Chinese thugs at a time. It doesn't help that her fighting style includes frequent acrobatic back-flips that just look silly. My favorite part is when a henchman stops in mid-melee to twirl his fancy multi-bladed knives in a gratuitous display of showboating before resuming the fight.

Posing as a bad-ass looking for action, Jackson infiltrates a powerful heroin smuggling ring with absurd ease. This Chinese syndicate is incongruously led by an American drug lord – Sid (Ken Metcalf), a dapper white dude who looks and behaves like a college professor – and his black henchman, Charlie (Stan Shaw). Jackson seduces Charlie and some dated jive-talk dialogue ensues. After several shoot-outs, an abduction, and a few more fights, the story winds down with a totally predictable ending.

Although I'm no stranger to no-budget schlock, the incredibly inept, careless production and ultra-cheap look of this film was almost insulting. The grainy, faded film stock and murky lighting has the unappealing ambience of a 16mm porn loop shot in someone's living room. This movie makes FOXY BROWN look like a glittering, big-budget masterpiece by comparison. If only it was bad enough to be enjoyed as camp.

The attraction to the Blaxploitation and martial arts genres is the lure of a fast-moving story with some exciting action. Although TNT JACKSON fails to deliver on that promise, it has two entertaining scenes that almost threaten to redeem the film. There is a pretty good cat-fight shot in a cemetery with Jackson beating up bitchy white girl Elaine (Pat Anderson), the drug lord's girlfriend. The other sequence – the only thing people remember from this film – takes a page out of the Shaw Brothers' book (the chapter on topless fight scenes). In a dark, woefully under-lit bedroom, a captive Jackson – wearing only a pair of black bikini briefs – breaks free and kicks the crap out of the goons who have abducted her. An almost iconic scene. Don't be surprised if Tarantino does an homage some day.

The acting is uniformly mediocre. Bell's flat, featureless performance makes one appreciate Pam Grier all the more. Grier generated a charisma and sex appeal that jumped off the screen, even when the scripts were terrible – and they usually were. Although Bell is lovely to look at, especially in her two obligatory nude scenes, her personality and acting skills are as bland as steamed rice.

Cirio H. Santiago would go on to direct more multiracial adventures such as THE MUTHERS (again with Jeannie Bell), EBONY, IVORY & JADE (both 1976), and a long string of low-budget action and women-in-prison films, mostly shot in The Philippines. – *Jim Ivers*

Colonel Faulkner (Sir Richard Burton) sprays hot lead in the 1970s action classic THE WILD GEESE.

THE WILD GEESE (1978/Severin)

Ever since I first saw it on NBC's Sunday Night Movie in 1982, I have loved THE WILD GEESE. The type of large scale action drama that THE EXPENDABLES wants to be but can't because it approaches its topic with too much self-aware humor, you'll nary find a better movie from an era when respected, acclaimed actors like Richard Burton and Richard Harris starred in such escapism. And this is why Severin's Blu-ray/DVD combo is a much appreciated release.

The mercenary-led warfare in the Congo of the 1960s and 70s has surprisingly inspired few movies, other than the fantastic DARK OF THE SUN, but THE WILD GEESE brings us a Dirty Dozen-style adventure of assembling the gonzo team of mostly middle-aged, misfit commandos recruited by Burton's character to rescue a deposed leader imprisoned by Simbas. After their benefactors doublecross them, the mercs are stranded in the Congo, hunted by Simbas and all hell breaks loose.

While some politically sensitive viewers may shirk at the use of apartheid-era South African film crews, to its credit, the movie doesn't shy away from racial politics of the region and is critical of South African policies. Talent from the 007 movies are shared, with a title sequence by Maurice Binder, 2nd unit action helmed by John Glen and Roger Moore as the team's pilot specialist. Moore, always a better actor in non-Bond films, has a blast chewing a cigar while engaging in tactical shooting, like a limey Sgt. Fury.

American helmer Andrew V. McLaglen (who passed away in August 2014) is not remembered as a great director by any means, but he was a solid crafter of adventure movies, despite overlong roadshow programmers like SHENANDOAH and some solid John Wayne vehicles like MCLINTOCK! and CHISUM. THE WILD GEESE is his best film, as he directs the material with straightforward, meat and potatoes aplomb.

Richard Burton is just fantastic as Colonel Alan Faulkner, realizing how much we've been cheated by the downgrade of acting in action films since the 1980s. With his screen presence, Welsh accent and the type of awesome, gravelly voice you only get from smoking cigarettes since age 8, Burton raises what might have been a *Boy's Own* adventure under any other actor to a sort of majestic level. Richard Harris, always seeming to fight a hangover, sports hilarious giant glasses with a cigarette dangling out of his mouth to inject some humor into his character, the single father who doesn't get to spend Xmas with his son because he chose the fight in the Congo.

Severin wisely carries over bonus features from prior DVD releases, and new interviews with the film's technical advisor "Mad" Mike Hoare, a legendary mercenary from the actual Congo conflicts, and director McLaglen, who swears that Burton and Harris did not drink booze while filming. Considering the legend that Richard Burton's autopsy revealed a spine crystallized in alcohol, that story is the hardest to believe. You also get a behind-the-scenes documentary short and audio commentary from Sir Roger Moore himself. Severin's new transfer is as good as expected. Any fan of this movie can consider this the definitive release. And if you've yet to see this film, you can't call yourself an action movie fan until you see Richard Burton wield an Uzi.

An international hit in 1978, it was acquired by the soon-to-be-defunct Allied Artists in America, where it had a disappointing run. But the film was given high profile network tv showings by both ABC and NBC when that meant much more than it does today.

Unfortunately, action movie lovers were deprived of a series of adventures featuring Colonel Alan Faulkner and his mercenaries. Burton died just one week before filming of THE WILD GEESE 2 commenced, where he was to reprise his role. Edward Fox stepped in to play a replacement character. – *John Grace*

HOTEL INFERNO (2014/Necrostorm)

After tackling the demented revenge film (ADAM CHAPLIN: VIOLENT AVENGER) and sci-fi/action/horror (TAETER CITY), the guys at Necrostorm are back with the first-person-shooter-inspired HOTEL INFERNO, an action/horror flick recommended for an "adult and conscious audience for private use."

When soldier-turned-hitman Frank Zimosa accepts a job from a mysterious agency fronted by the equally mysterious Mistrandia (who is never seen but communicates via earpiece or television), it seems straightforward, if a tad messy sounding. Booked into a luxury hotel by his employer, he's instructed to "smash the skulls and extract the brain... open the stomach and remove the guts" of the couple staying in the next room.

Outfitted by the agency with a pair of wearable tech a la Google Glass, Zimosa sets out to complete his mission but quickly realizes that all is not what it seems. His targets turn out to be agency employees that have outlived their usefulness, a situation that the faux software engineer (his cover story for the galpal he calls throughout the flick) soon finds himself facing.

While other flicks have flirted with the first-person-shooter perspective, HOTEL INFERNO – directed by TAETER CITY'S Giulio DeSanti – proclaims itself as the first to embrace the concept from start to finish. And who am I to argue? (Though, as David Z pointed out, the flick does bear a passing resemblance to the 2012 videogame CONDEMNED 2: BLOOD SHOT right down to the talking television.)

But were HOTEL INFERNO to employ the unique perspective simply as a device for a glorified cinematic video game, it might wear out its welcome long before its 80-minute running time is up. As it is, one long, silent, aggressively violent stretch featuring Zimosa's attempt to escape the woods surrounding the hotel feels like it was lifted right from one of the videogames that critics are (once again) suggesting turn gamers into homicidal maniacs.

Fortunately, De Santi (who also produced the flick and supervised the visual effects) recognizes the limitations of such a device and infuses HOTEL INFERNO with a Lovecraftian influence that gives the story some third act "oomph" it might have otherwise lacked. And the director never flinches, employing the first-person perspective to good effect whether it's blasting away at agency flunkies, blowing chunks in a hotel sink, taking a knife to the hand or trying to avoid a centuries-old monster patrolling the hotel's halls.

Certainly the most interesting premise of the three Necrostorm flicks, HOTEL INFERNO does suffer from some stiff dubbing but De Santi wisely branches out from TAETER CITY's almost fetishized emphasis on head violence with some inspired low-budget mayhem. (The DVD includes a crash course on how some of the paint-the-screen-red splatter effects were achieved.) And like its predecessors, De Santi keeps the running time at a tight sub-90-minutes which prevents boredom from creeping in even when the middle act sags a bit.

I'm not sure if these Necrostorm flicks are outliers or are the leading edge of a new Spaghetti Splatter movement, but each flick delivers its own unique take on a classic cinematic trope (revenge flick, sci-fi statement, shoot-'em-up hijinks) that makes them a worthy addition to any gorehound's shelf – and HOTEL INFERNO is no exception. – *Dan Taylor*

For more reviews of action, horror, sci-fi and sleaze be sure to visit Dantenet.com and ERonline.blogspot.com

ER #52 :: page 44

LANCASTER-PLOITATION

by John Grace

At the 2013 Denver Comic Convention, legendary artist Jim Steranko was asked who was the toughest guy he knew. Steranko, who socialized and worked with many Hollywood greats as a storyboard artist and publisher of Mediascene/Prevue, started talking about Burt Lancaster. Lancaster, an imposing presence at 6'1" and possessing an athlete's physique, was said to be quite a bully. Picking on cast members, directors, producers and crew members, Burt could be really mean, the biggest bully in Hollywood....

"Burt would pick on Kirk Douglas, calling him 'shorty,'" Steranko said. "But then Burt worked with my friend Richard Brooks."

On the set of ELMER GANTRY, Burt said the wrong words to Richard Brooks, and according to Steranko, Brooks knocked Burt right the fuck out. Lancaster straightened his act up for the rest of the shoot.

Lancaster is one of those classic Hollywood era actors that always represented strength and smarts, but often conflicted introspection. In the 1970s, too old to continue the leading roles that made him famous (from CRIMSON PIRATE, THE TRAIN, CRISS CROSS and numerous others), Lancaster was said to be doing films for his own artistic satisfaction, not financial reasons. Could also be that Burt's bully reputation made him not such a desirable stateside talent. In other words, lots of independent and foreign work in the filmography.

Raro Video continues their superb line of under-appreciated Italian films from the 60s and 70s with an excellent release of Lancaster re-teaming with Luchino Visconti, GRUPPO DI FAMIGLIA IN UN INTERNO, or as the English speaking world calls it, CONVERSATION PIECE. Their first collaboration was the classic 1963 film THE LEOPARD. CONVERSATION PIECE is not so classic.

In a role reflecting the director's weakened, post-stroke physical state of the time, Lancaster stars as a retired professor renting his Rome apartments to

Lancaster as Il Professore in Luchino Visconti's CONVERSATION PIECE (1974).

a vulgar, obnoxious assortment of characters, namely the leftist revolutionary and ladies man played by Helmut Berger. Berger was Visconti's lover, so the director's camera obsesses over the actor, who chews scenery quite a bit.

Most of the film is Lancaster's character stressing over arguments and confrontations with his tenants. This isn't exactly spine-tingling, ER standard stuff, and often seems like an SCTV satire of a pretentious Italian art film. The dinner finale has the left winger Berger arguing a right winger in silly, one-dimensional polemics that made the film a laughing stock in its day.

Not well-received in its original release – but like most famous director's failures – CONVERSATION PIECE has a cult of appreciators. Lancaster handles his role with dignity, although not dominating the scenes like you want him to. I found too many unintentional laughs, particularly the explosive fate of Berger's vexatious radical, to take the film with too much weight or sincerity. Your own mileage may vary. Visconti died not long after the movie was released, making the epilogue of a terminally ill Lancaster sadder than intended.

Raro's transfer is excellent, with those deep, rich colors you only see in Italian scoped films of the 60s and 70s, and making Visconti's limited, soundstage apartment sets look so much nicer. Visconti was disabled at the time, so he wanted very limited locations. English language audio track is your only option, but you'll want to hear Lancaster's voice.

And from the depressing and unintentionally camp to the type of rollicking adventure we want to see Burt star in, Severin brings us a much appreciated Blu-Ray/DVD combo release of ZULU DAWN, the 1979 followup to ZULU. The type of big-budget widescreen adventure no longer made in Western civilization, ZULU DAWN is a large scale depiction of one of the British Empire's great military losses, the Battle of Isandlwana, the first major conflict of the Zulu Kingdom and the British Empire and the worst defeat of the British military by a native population in history.

Lancaster portrays Anthony Durnford, the Natal Native Contingent Captain. The real Durnford was Irish-born, but Burt's accent waivers between an attempted Irish brogue and an intercontinental accent. Still, you get the sense Burt had it in his contract to look noble and cool in every scene. Lancaster gets the definitive "ain't going out like a bitch" death scene, as he knocks out Zulu attackers with his rifle butt while standing Frazetta-like on a wagon. The legend takes a bullet and his stuntman takes a wince-worthy fall off a cliff. Definitely in the Lancaster contract.

I vaguely recall a prominent zine editor writing off this film as pro-apartheid propaganda, making one wonder if the editor actually watched the movie. The British troops, led by Lord Chelmsford (played by Peter O'Toole, also in a post-stardom slump), are portrayed as foolish, stubborn, arrogant, sloppy and not all that bright. The Zulus are portrayed as noble defenders of their land, responding to a bullying empire. By the time 1000s of Zulus charge over the hill at the stuffy Brits, you find yourself rooting for them.

Director Douglas Hickox has a sad pre-battle sequence where a young flag boy is killed by friendly fire, just in case you needed to be reminded who to cheer for. And the battle is depicted in sweeping, large scale violence and mayhem, the type you can't see these days without a majority of CGI painting.

There are rumors that Hickox's work was mostly reshot by 2nd Unit Directors Peter MacDonald and David Tomblin. MacDonald later took over the directing reigns on RAMBO III after Stallone fired Russell Mulcahy, so it foreshadowed his career. O'Toole was said to be a problem on the set, but no word on Burt bullying anybody. Other cast members include Simon Ward, Ronald Lacey and, because he must always be the obligatory loudmouth commander in any British movie (or seems to be), the recently-deceased Bob Hoskins.

Those keeping track of the late Ken Gampu's film roles in nearly every feature shot in the continent (and fans of his work in the Shotokansploitation classic KILL AND KILL AGAIN) will note that he portrays the traitor Mantshonga.

ZULU DAWN is thrilling, big screen fun that is lovingly presented by Severin. Bonus features include interviews with historian/author Ian Knight (who visits the real locations of the battle in a featurette) and the film's Historical Advisor Midge Carter. A big budget flop in 1979, ZULU DAWN holds up better than some of the "weightier" hits of the era.

Interestingly, after ZULU DAWN bombed, Peter O'Toole starred in Richard Rush's THE STUNTMAN, cementing his career comeback and new critical respect.

Lancaster starred in Louis Malle's much-loved ATLANTIC CITY, getting his career out of a slump. But frankly, I'd rather watch a blood and thunder epic like ZULU DAWN than either actor's comeback vehicles.

Whether exploitation, Canadian tax shelter, or ill-thought out foreign production, Burt Lancaster was always an actor worth watching. Seeing what he could bring to what might otherwise be perceived as an undignified role is an essential part of a film viewing appreciation.

John Grace wrote about MEMPHIS HEAT and the 60s spy flick LICENSED TO KILL in ER 51. He is one of the hosts of The Midnight Movie Cowboys podcast. For info visit midnightmoviecowboys. podbean.com or find them on Facebook.

For more reviews of action, horror, sci-fi and sleaze be sure to visit Dantenet.com and ERonline.blogspot.com

In the Next Exploitation Retrospect

WANTED: MACK BOLAN

Exploitation Retrospect continues its look at the world of men's action novels with a spotlight on the hugely popular series THE EXECUTIONER featuring Mack Bolan. Plus, Remo Williams in other media, paperback/trash sinema reviews and much more.

Did you miss ER 51 featuring Barbara Steele, the porn/wrestling connection, Kinski in NOSFERATU IN VENICE, Bruno Mattei and more? Copies of EXPLOITATION RETROSPECT #51 are still available in limited quantities for $6 (US) and $9 (international). Visit dantenet.com/er/about/revenge.html for ordering info or send **cash only** to PO Box 5531, Lutherville, MD 21094-5531.

ER #52 :: page 47

Empire of the Apes (see page 63)

REVIEWS

REPLIGATOR (2013/Whacked Movies)

The first time I heard of REPLIGATOR was at a recent *Cinema Wasteland*. I missed the screening and now wish I had seen this in a packed room.

The basic premise is that a scientist invents a teleportation device. Works great, except when you send men through it they turn into hot girls. If you send ugly girls into it they turn into hot girls. In other words: Best. Invention. Ever. The government wants the teleporter to work properly so they enlist the aid of another scientist who has invented a brainwashing program. He incorporates the brainwashing program into the teleporter so at least the hot girls do what you say.

Small problem. The brainwashing program utilizes a technology that stimulates the brain stem where the lizard in all of us lives. The primordial soup, so to speak. Now, if the hot girls have sex they turn into alligator women and kill. And, if that wasn't enough, the people it kills get up and... well, they become gay and want to have gay sex.

What can I say? This movie is genius.

It comes off like a classic piece of sexploitation with incredible, naked women. The monsters are of the really cool, rubber-suited variety and Gunnar Hansen and Brinke Stevens are in it! How could you go wrong?

The correct answer is, you can't.

The entire time I watched it I thought it had a 90's feel to it. Guess I watch too many movies because it was originally shot in 1996. Bret McCormick, director of the twisted THE ABOMINATION (1986) shows up to do a little interview and there is a behind-the-scenes feature from when the film was originally shot.

REPLIGATOR is a fun little jaunt back in time to when movies could just be silly fun. – *Douglas A. Waltz*

SEXCULA (1974/Impulse Pictures)

Nothing sets the hearts of trash film geeks aflutter quite like the news of a "lost film" unearthed from some dank and musty vault. Just the idea of such talk takes me back to my tape-trading days of the 1980s when word of a long-forgotten Spaghetti Western or underground European splatterfest would keep the US Postal Service and blank VHS suppliers in the black for weeks as tapes shot across the country and around the world for curious eyes to see.

So when Impulse Pictures announced that they were releasing SEXCULA, an elusive slice of 70s North-of-the-Bordersploitation "transferred from the rare theatrical print stored in the basement of the Library and Archives of Canada" even *my* long-dormant sick flick radar started going haywire.

Unfortunately, one viewing was all it took to remind me that sometimes lost... is better. (Apologies to Stephen King.)

Playing like a dementoid, over-sexed Canuck version of LADY FRANKENSTEIN, SEXCULA

ER #52 :: page 48

features Debbie Collins as a young woman who brings her boyfriend (screenwriter David Hurry) to the old family castle and promises to relate stories that will "curl your pubes". One naked picnic later we're being treated to tales of Baroness Fellatingstein (Jamie Orlando), a curvy scientist with a problem. Seems as though her latest creation – John Alexander as "Frank" – is cursed with "sleeping sex cells" and isn't interested in pleasuring her.

Cue Countess Sexcula (Collins again), a tan (?!) vampiress who is more than happy to answer the call and help the Baroness. (And when I say "answer the call" I mean it. Even though we're told that SEXCULA takes place in 1869 the Countess has a mid-70s phone in her boudoir, a full seven years before Alexander Graham Bell declared "Mr. Watson, come here… I want to see you".)

Armed with a deep, abiding interest in erotic health and sexual healing, Countess Sexcula sets about diagnosing and attempting to cure Frank's dormant dong through a series of hardcore vignettes featuring everything from a burly lumberjack and a horny drunk to a porn film studio wedding that turns into an orgy.

Unfortunately, and perhaps predictably, it's the sex scenes that bring SEXCULA screeching to a halt (especially the endless wedding orgy). Your fast forward button is likely to get as much of a workout as some of the Canuck beaver on display throughout this bizzaro sinematic artifact.

Despite the Catskills lodge humor and stilted cue card readings from the female leads, the flick's non-sex scenes have a certain, undeniable charm. And when John Alexander is around, SEXCULA's wasted potential is on full display. His take on the flaccid Frankenstein is the film's highlight, with the "monster" portrayed as a dopey, fey, undersexed goofball who would rather have Sexcula make him a sandwich than suck his… well, you know. He's like a low-rent Dick Shawn and seems to be having a grand old time throughout even when his dick is flapping around as he chases Sexcula, Fellatingstein and another cutie through a field.

Not quite successful as a horror spoof and certainly not titillating enough for a porno, SEXCULA unfortunately comes up short on all counts. Too bad director John Holbrook (billed here as Bob Hollowich) didn't go all in on more of the flick's offbeat components like the bizarre stripper/ape bump & grind, the horny hunchback or the telepathic sex robot. Had he fully embraced the idea of SEXCULA as a horror spoof maybe it would be more deserving of the "lost cult classic" label. – Dan Taylor

BATH SALT ZOMBIES (2012/MVD)

I miss the days of topical exploitation and horror cinema, when filmmakers would rip their storylines right from the headlines to offer up slightly (or more than slightly) fictionalized tales of the day's news events. Whether they were showing us the horrors of marijuana (REEFER MADNESS), teen pregnancy (TEENAGE MOTHER), cults (GUAYAN: CULT OF THE DAMNED) or savage dictators (THE RISE AND FALL OF IDI AMIN), trash filmmakers could often be counted upon to scare up some sort of cinematic boogieman that would make our own lives seem safe and tame by comparison.

Then again, after watching BATH SALT ZOMBIES maybe it's just a whole hell of a lot easier to rip-off the SAW and PARANORMAL ACTIVITY flicks.

Inspired by the wave of "bath salt"-related violent crimes and cannibalistic behavior, BATH SALT ZOMBIES feels like it wants to be this generation's answer to the aforementioned REEFER MADNESS. It even starts with a *faux* bath salts health class propaganda video, though I don't recall any of the 16mm flicks I saw in high school being peppered with profanity, face-eating and an appearance by Satan himself.

Once that's out of the way (and it's not half as funny as you'd hope a profane parody complete with Satanic cameo would be) the plot jumps to present day NYC where it appears that about twenty people live. Ritchie (Brandon Salkil) and his bitchy, busty girlfriend Angel (Erin Ryan) are strung-out junkies in search of their next high until Ritchie scores some new smokeable bath salts from Bubbles (Ethan Holey), a biz-savvy dealer willing to give away that first pack for free.

Little does Ritchie know that he'll not only be instantly hooked on the junk, but the military-grade designer drug will also turn him into a twitchy, super-strong monster with a proclivity for killing gals with big, natural boobs.

From there BSZ ping-pongs from Ritchie and his killing sprees to the DEA agent on his tail, to Bubbles and drug designer Sal (affably played by director Dustin Wayde Mills) complete with headache-inducing shaky-cam, comically grotesque makeup that gets more outrageous as the flick progresses and a couple flashes of not-quite-brilliance that made me wonder what could have been.

Made for less than a day's catering on TWI-LIGHT, the micro-budget strains the production at the seams, highlighting both its pluses (a couple good performances, some inspired stylized mayhem) and minuses (a handful of bad performances, video-gamey CGI, flat script). Salkil makes a fine, twitchy junkie-monster and seems to be having a good time, especially during two over-the-top slaughter rampages that highlight the flick. Unfortunately, much of the flick's 70-minute running time is monopolized by Josh Eal's shouting DEA agent, who lays waste to drug cookers and doughnuts with equal aplomb.

With its mix of punk rock music (and filmmaking), face-ripping gore, "real" actors, junkie atmosphere and zero budget, BATH SALT ZOMBIES comes off like some bastard lovechild of the Cinema of Transgression and HG Lewis. Which is probably just enough of an endorsement for me to give Mills' NIGHT OF THE TENTACLES (also starring Salkil and Mills) a whirl. – *Dan Taylor*

BONG OF THE DEAD (2010/ Horizon Motion Pictures)

Zombie movies are pervasive enough to factor audience assumptions into their storytelling. Shots to the head, brain-eating, slow shuffling; we hold these truths to be self-evident. Similarly, we accept that the foolish might not only survive, but be rewarded with truly bad-ass chicks for their efforts. (That some of the zombies are downright chatty might not, however, be as palatable to genre purists.)

In BONG OF THE DEAD, Tommy (Jy Harris) and Edwin (Mark Wynn) have ridden out the zombie apocalypse baked, perhaps a perfectly sensible response to the circumstances. (The line between empathizing and mockery is thin for the sober viewer.) So inebriated, they make a logic leap which leads to a Monsanto-worthy moment of marijuana magic. As suspension of disbelief rules in the land of the dead, why can't reanimated brains be the secret ingredient for fertilizing some truly fine bud? There's also a lot of horsing around during the end of the world; this movie could be twenty minutes tighter, but it's a drug comedy. Hijinks had during their meandering road trip to obtain more zombie gray matter for whipping up their green goo are perfectly permissible. Along the way, they acquire Leah (Simone Bailly), an aggressive, shotgun-toting, Sarah Connor-inspired beauty straight out of a teenage boy's Sci-Fi dreams.

BONG OF THE DEAD melds stoner comedy to the overdone zombi-com genre with damned admirable results, especially for a film which reportedly cost only five thousand dollars to make. Most of us would be applauded to come up with the prologue (a charming silent film-like sequence involving an elderly couple of lawn gnome enthusiasts at the heart of the outbreak) for that much money.

This is movie effects make-up artist Thomas Newman's first film as director, not to mention writer, editor, cinematographer, producer, composer and jack of all trades. It should lead him to bigger things. Everything about this concept is fraught with pitfalls leading straight into truly bad movie territory, and instead he's created a very watchable, entertaining flick. Not only is every penny on screen, he wrings from each buck about a grand's worth of results. Budget limitations have been overcome with style and humor, proving vision and drive can always triumph. (Only the dubbed audio stands out as a distraction.) His solution for how to shower after the zombie-fueled breakdown of society and THE A-TEAM meets DEAD ALIVE zombie-killing truck are both genius. Most importantly for a film made by an effects man, the gore here is fantastic; testament to both his skill and evident ability to get ingredients wholesale. The blood and latex flies in copious quantities. As Newman's one-man-band production, BONG OF THE DEAD is an enjoyable success. All that's missing is a contact buzz. – *Jay Kulpa*

RUDYARD KIPLING'S MARK OF THE BEAST (2012/Blood Bath Pictures)

Fleete (Phil Hall) and Debbie (the unstoppable Debbie Rochon) join Maggie (Margaret Rose Champagne) and her friend Natalie (Ellen Muth) at the lakeside cabin of Sheriff Denny (Dick Boland) and Sheri (Sherri Lynn) Strickland for a New Year's Eve bash with a gang of other friends.

There is talk of strange people living in a temple in the woods, a temple where they "worship that beast monkey god," and the people at the strange party (strange because it really is kind of small and out of the way, and aside from loads of hooch the only real attraction seems to be a homemade spinning-top-haunted-house game) get pretty strange themselves. Particularly Fleete, who completes his revelry by throwing the host's car keys into the river and vomiting in bed.

While being trundled back after an aborted attempt at stumbling home, Fleete makes the grave mistake of dishonoring a random woodland shrine to the monkey god. For which he is promptly punished by the sudden appearance of a ragged, bandaged and (we're informed) diseased figure whose malformed ass promptly attacks and bites the drunken infidel. And then disappears. This bodes ill for all, as Strickland and the other locals seem to have a fearful sort of respect for the monkey god people.

Fleete becomes sick almost immediately, developing a hankering for rare meat and a buckshot scattering of black sores on his chest. The wise Sheriff thinks the fellow might just be cursed, and he might just be right as Fleete is allowed to take a bite out of Maggie's arm. Cue drama of splitting up, running around, and more of the dramatic narration that's been plaguing us since the beginning.

Tied to a chair, Fleete is pronounced possessed by Denny despite "the doctor" at a conveniently vague location nearby opining that it looks like rabies. A comically half-assed exorcism takes place, based on the Bible story of the Legion and the pigs, with worms being tossed at the sick man in an attempt to draw out his demons. This devolves into an argument, then a philosophy session, and melodrama flares as the "silver leper" howls in the woods and blue light shines into the cabin.

The next tactic is to go out into the woods with sticks and convince the leper to come back to the cabin and lift the curse. Somehow the creature is subdued and tied up as well for what turns into a parody of some gangland interrogation: a hot poker and great quantities of pompous narration and crass dialogue are used to burn the silver leper repeatedly. The creature gibbers and moans, and finally everybody gets tired of it all and the thing is untied to crawl over to Fleete's lap and, apparently, dismiss his vexation before collapsing.

There's some powerful bad rumination; with some token first aid and a few accusatory looks the leper just sort of totters off into the woods; furniture is moved back into place (after an earlier messy fit involving perhaps the film's most apt scene, in which a director's chair is tossed carelessly aside); there's a parable about how to deal with them damn native superstitions; and, as Sheriff Strickland himself says at one point, "As long as I live I will never talk about this night again." Good call.

And that's my patience, finished. I'd been looking forward to this too, if for nothing other than the appearance of (as I believe I've referred to her before) adorable gremlin-faced Ellen Muth, not seen by this viewer since the fine short-lived series DEAD LIKE ME. And while she may be kindly slumming here (although not too kindly not to require a personal assistant), she really doesn't add much to the proceedings.

A fairly rich dramatic score by Glen Gabriel is poorly met with the stilted voiceover by Rochon, the attempt to blend Kipling's 19th century dialogue into this 21st century take-off being... unsuccessful. Lakeside yuppies trying to get Biblical does not play well here, and while I never say this, the peeling poster board characters resort to saying "fuck" way too often in an attempt the heighten the seriousness of their useless statements. Time of day and geographic location are shuffled into near-meaninglessness throughout, a muddling effect assisted by a generally flat atmosphere provided by tight sets and discombobulating camera work substituting for scenery. The "silver leper" is kind of cool-looking though (makeup by Leigh Radziwon), like a mole person crossed with a bad potato. Wrapped in soiled cheesecloth. (No, not being sarcastic there, it is effectively freaky.)

The DVD comes with extras such as "Behind the Scenes" scenes, trailers and director's commentary. Well, I'm getting paid the same whether I review the extras or not, and since none of them appear to offer the promise of footage of the Personal Assistant to Ms. Muth shaving her pits, I'm gonna skip 'em. (Well, all right, I skimmed "Behind the Scenes"; no dice.) Instead I tried to find Rudyard Kipling's original tale MARK OF THE BEAST online and see just how badly they managed to torture a short story by stretching it out on a 72-minute rack (don't have it in my library, wasn't moved to wade through Camp Snoopy outside the public library to find it). And here it is: http://www.readbookonline.net/readOnLine/2420/. A classic 1890 horror story so much richer in detail, tighter yet more well-developed, and simply more fantastic and alarming than the film. In a free form that will take you less time to read than it will to watch. I'd suggest doing just that. – Crites

EDITOR'S NOTE: *It's with great sadness and regret that I include the previous review from longtime ER contributor Tom Crites. Better known simply as "Crites", Tom wrote for both ER and our sister publication/site The Hungover Gourmet for many years. We shared a love of trash cinema, zines and grub so it seemed natural that we'd eventually hook up. I never met Tom in person or even spoke to him on the phone but we exchanged emails and recipes, dining notes and pork rind/film reviews. Lengthy silences on his end weren't unusual and though I'd come to expect them they always made me nervous. In the summer of 2013 my worst fears were realized and I received an email from his family that Tom had passed away. Always prolific and dependable, I have a folder of contributions from him on my desktop. I'm sure some will find their way into the zine, blog or site over time, but this was one of his final contributions and I'll always remember his gung-ho spirit, whether it was for a trashy horror DVD or some dish he wanted to rave about. To paraphrase the way he signed many emails and notes over the years, "take it easy Crites".*

DISCO EXORCIST (2012/Wild Eye)

What is the cut-off for historical costume drama? THE DISCO EXORCIST wears all the trappings to reenact a Seventies drive-in movie, from the Grindhouse-style effects that "damage the print" to the clothes, pacing, and score. The hair (especially lead Michael Reed's wig) is never quite right, and the stage blood is of too recent a vintage, but a lot of love went into capturing the style. There are exceptions, but the naked girls snorting coke with our "dashing" stud of a protagonist, Rex Romanski, can be forgiven their blue and pink hair.

The jokes are pretty painful, usually in the style of "hey this is a Seventies spoof, remember Quaaludes? Do a bump!" When lothario Rex (Reed) meets Rita (Ruth Sullivan) at the disco, it's supposed to be understood that this is just a one night stand, free-love-style. (Rita even overhears her own trio of "witches" warning not to get involved, so really only has herself to blame.) So when he throws her over for Porn Star Amoreena Jones (Sarah Nicklin) the very next night, Rita overreacts, pitching a fit worthy of Carrie at the prom, and makes with the cursin'. While Amoreena recruits Rex build the porn and nose candy-fueled relationship of their dreams, Rita decides to snatch some porn souls, raise the dead, and massacre an orgy.

Director Richard Griffin has made several light and entertaining horror-comedies, including SPLATTER DISCO (complete with a musical number), and here displays a deft, crowd-pleasing touch. DISCO EXORCIST has a pretty full plate of nudity, silly sex, and comic relief characters. It feels like a high-concept, spoof-trailer made for Youtube that somehow got bankrolled into a full feature, but also a labor of love. Vulgar, over the top and trying too hard at times, this is a Saturday night exploitation lovers' delight that'll leave a smile on your face. I, for one, will definitely be seeking out more of Griffin's work. – Jay Kulpa

EVERYONE MUST DIE (2012/MVD)

The flick opens with a slasher working through a town slaughtering folks. Then Kyle's sister gets killed and it gets personal. He discovers that the killer must be unstoppable as he killed him. Then he figures out the pattern as the killer cuts a bloody swath across the country. Going from one small town to another and leaving a body count in his wake.

Kyle figures out the killer's next target and decides it's time to end this once and for all.

EVERYONE MUST DIE takes the slasher genre and embraces it. We know when we see a bunch of kids at a backyard barbeque that they are in for a rough night. We get the slutty girl and she even gets naked. We get the sweet girl and she is gorgeous and doesn't get naked. See! It follows the rules.

And then it does this thing. This thing that can not be revealed for it would spoil the discovery. The discovery of what may be the purest form of genius I have encountered since becoming a fan of the slasher genre waaaaay back in the 80s. This is what makes this movie completely different from all the others. ALL THE OTHERS! I can not stress this enough.

Sure, we have the classics and they will always be the classics, but the new wave of slasher flicks just came across as tired same old same old. Sure, once in a while you get something original like Dave Campfield's CAESAR AND OTTO'S SUMMER CAMP MASSACRE, but that happens pretty far and few.

EVERYONE MUST DIE takes its ending and turns the game on its ear. When you see what it is you will ask yourself why no one had ever thought of this before.

Ah, it's good to know that someone has the slasher love and brought a whole new dimension to the game.

Thanks EVERYONE MUST DIE. Now, for the cold hard truth. With what you have set up here you MUST deliver. There MUST be another one. It MUST take what you have given us here and expound upon it. We MUST get more of what you have teased us with. Failure to do this might result in being forever shamed in the horror community.

In simpler terms: don't fuck this up.

Oh, and the movie is awesome and you must watch it. In case that wasn't made clear with the previous rant. – Douglas A. Waltz

DEAD CERT (2010/Shout Factory)

First off, this is not the posh 1974 DEAD CERT, a Tony Richardson adaptation of a Dick Francis mystery staring Dame Judi Dench. Nope. This is more a chav, "Guy Ritchie's FROM DUSK TILL DAWN," a shot-on-video mash-up of Boxers, British Gangsters, and a competing gang who happen to be Vampires. They just happen to be Cockney instead of sparkly.

Freddy Frankham is a nice, wholesome London Gangster trying to start a family with his girlfriend while managing her boxer brother. Opening a small Gentlemen's Club in an old warehouse, he's a bad man making good and no one understands him like his woman. During the rather sad opening night, Dante Livienko shows up with his sociopathic crew. They aren't messing around (except for with the dancers), as they want to take over the bar, the local drug trade, and are vampires, to boot. Settling things over boxing doesn't do it, so will a fully-fanged defense of the club do it when the good guys come to take it back?

There really is nothing more to this than half a London Gangster movie mated with the FROM DUSK movies. Smushed together, they actually cancel out each others' crackle. Know the old adage "when you show a gun in the first act, it has to go off in the third?" Well, they do that here early on in a manner that should become thuddingly obvious to, if not the attentive viewer, at least me. It makes the build to the climax more of a "oh, hurry up already" than a "well, isn't that clever" when you know from the git-go what'll stop the Vamps.

Former Bond-baddie and TV-Hitler Steven Berkoff plays the Van Helsing here, while Billy Murray is Livienko. Craig Fairbrass is the world's most cockney protagonist, while Danny Dyer, Dexter Fletcher, and Jason Flemyng show up as vaguely familiar faces to anyone who catches their fair share of British TV and cinema. Wavering audio levels don't help the thick accents while the serious lack of bloodshed won't satisfy the gore fans. An even greater offense is the complete lack of nudity in a b-movie set in a Gentlemen's Club. All these Gangsters, and that's the only real crime committed here.

At some point while watching DEAD CERT, you'll also be asking "Why the hell is this on Blu-Ray?" Shot with a RED One camera, this movie looks great but there's something about it that stands out as being very "video." 1080P and 7.1 audio aren't always kind (the dialogue is unintelligible in places), but do emphasize how RED's digital recording captures light and detail beautifully. I say "just embrace that and move on, because while it don't look great, 'tis the camera of the future."

A painless, stylish, utterly unmemorable 90 minutes. – *Jay Kulpa*

GROUND ZERO (2011/Shock-O-Rama)

Zombie movies are the new ninja movies. Their popularity in this day and age has made them a dime a dozen. The only way to really stand out from the crowd is to either be really damn good or have an interesting new take on a very old, over-saturated genre. Sadly GROUND ZERO doesn't really do either of these things.

Political activist Darius Hendricks (Brian Sheets) breaks into Nat-Tech Corp to steal a top secret chemical. He injects himself with it and goes into hiding, planning to document the effects of the chemical and expose Nat-Tech Corp but all does not go according to plan and Nat-Tech Corp hunts Darius down.

Enter Jarius (Mike Langer) who seems to have a never ending supply of women troubles and Greer (Sahna Foley) who has penchant for nice shoes. Jarius and Greer are two professional cleaners who are hired to clean up some bodies in a warehouse. They are given strict orders and a very strict timeframe which would net them a very big payday. Because of the amount of work involved they are joined by two bumbling goofs Jeff (D.L. Walker) and Ted (Chris Harvey) who were also hired by their employer. Things seem very routine at first until one of the dead bodies decides to rise from the grave.

Due to budget constraints GROUND ZERO tries to focus on how a zombie epidemic may start, which is fine, but the movie starts *literally* at ground zero and the lack of cast makes it hard to build tension and immediacy when only one zombie seems to come back at a time. A large part of GROUND ZERO takes place in an abandon warehouse with maybe four or five people in a room at a time. Everything comes off as small and frankly uninteresting. Most of the movie deals with the personal issues of the cleaners or failed attempts at comic relief. The flick moves at a snail's pace and even though the cleaners were given a strict timeline within which to do their massive job, there's no sense of time throughout the film. Everyone seems to be standing around talking or doing menial work like scrubbing up blood. Every once and a while these things are broken up by a zombie but even then it's uninteresting due to bad editing and choreography.

Jeff and Ted – the two bumbling cleaners who join the professionals – are the comic relief of the film, if you could call them that. They spend most of the movie referencing and impersonating beloved, over-referenced films like STAR WARS and THE LORD OF THE RINGS which just makes you want to turn GROUND ZERO off and put on a better film. As overplayed as the zombie genre can be so is making references to popular geek culture. The acting is serviceable and that is really all one can hope for when it comes to a very low budget zombie film.

Surprisingly, for such a low budget and seeming ineptitude in all other cinematic categories, the special effects are well executed. A mix of very simple practical effects and some CGI they're still not enough to save this film.

GROUND ZERO is just another zombie film in a sea of zombie films. It adds nothing to the genre and is dragged down by terrible pacing, barely serviceable acting, and a paper thin premise. It goes nowhere fast and in about the same time it will fade from your memory. – *Adam Knabe*

AN AMERICAN HIPPIE IN ISRAEL (1972/Grindhouse Releasing)

The rediscovery of "lost" films is always a boon to world of cinema, even if the newly found treasure isn't of the highest quality. Consider Rene Belloq's archeology example from RAIDERS OF THE LOST ARK; even the simplest trinket magnifies in values as it's lost, then discovered anew by future generations.

AN AMERICAN HIPPIE IN ISRAEL is Belloq's ten dollar silver pocket watch unearthed after nearly forty years, dusted off, then gussied up as a far more valuable relic. Grindhouse Releasing has erected a grandstand from which to proclaim the wonder of this peculiar anti-war piece, packing into a limited edition wrapper no less than three discs and a bevy of special features which will both amuse and confuse. What are cult fans getting themselves into though by biting off a piece of this hippie fairy tale?

AN AMERICAN HIPPIE IN ISRAEL is a monologue and folk song-heavy allegorical tale of one American wanderer's desperate attempt to cope with the horrors he experienced while pressed into service in Vietnam. Protagonist Mike arrives in Israel with few ambitions beyond escaping the horrors whirling at frappe speed across the plains of his psyche. In pursuit are a pair of murderous mimes whose only purpose appears to be tormenting Mike. While the film also makes true on the promises of strange robots (ripped straight from DIAMONDS ARE FOREVER if James Bond was dosed with LSD) and bloodthirsty sharks (whose temperament isn't actually gauged), the primary thrust of the film is comprised of hippie spinning, commune guitarmanship, and free loving about as erotic as nudist colony footage.

The majority of the run time sustains itself on long takes of hippies hanging out, traversing a beautiful desert landscape, and enjoying mellow cause rock. While the film is shot competently, it never transcends the cloud cover to become gorgeous. Despite all of this, I'm glad that it was rediscovered by western audiences. Below the peeling paint lies a serious message told with earnest fervor. There's a niche circuit for artistic message films which will positively eat this up. The surface anti-war message isn't the only philosophical discourse in play here; each time you've solved the Rubik's Cube, a new color is presented to challenge and engage. There's no reality where AN AMERICAN HIPPIE IN ISRAEL is mistaken for THE SEVENTH SEAL, but a compelling case could be made that it is THE SEVENTH SEAL through the earnest heart of Ed Wood. That sort of comparison could invite accusations that this is a stupid or bad film (and it has by some reviewers), but I would argue that such slander against Ed Wood and this film is tantamount to a breakdown in the linguistic framing used to relate cinematic experiences in the simplest terminology possible (even if it's incorrect).

AN AMERICAN HIPPIE IN ISRAEL is not a good film, but it is absolutely an interesting one.

In that way its preservation is important and its rediscovery a joyous occasion – even if the movie becomes mired in a peace-love bog from time to time. The best viewing experience possible requires an engaged audience; barring that a hip group of friends will suffice. If you have access to neither Grindhouse Releasing was kind enough to included an audio track of the film as an audiences experiences it – a very welcome addition for those without a repertoire or independent cinema house nearby. A bevy of interviews, features, and goodies pack out the limited edition release, including an uncut DVD of the director's other film THE HITCHHIKER.

AN AMERICAN HIPPIE IN ISRAEL is strange and peculiar, yet often inept with long stretches of hippie shenanigans. Those looking for an experience in allegorical madness have found their train station; those perpetually looking for another hit of cult crazy should snort this line of cinematic psychedelia; and those whose depth of "bad cinema" begins and ends with tangential references to Ed Wood should probably steer clear. – *Chuck Francisco*

DROPPING EVIL (2012/Wild Eye)

Back in 2011 Joss Whedon gave us a movie called CABIN IN THE WOODS. It took the basic 80s premise of camping gone horribly wrong and turned it on its ear. I watched it, thought it was alright. The monsters were cool and how often do you get to see a unicorn? In the end it felt flat to me.

DROPPING EVIL kind of takes that same approach. We get a group of teenagers that are going camping. They invite their Bible-thumping friend Nancy. It is important to realize that Nancy is a dude in this movie. Not sure why he was named Nancy, but that's not important. A brief note before we start. If you're going to have a guy playing a Bible-thumping Christian you're going to need to cover up his crappy tattoos. The character would never have had them.

Anyway, they go camping and one of them slips Nancy some LSD on the trip. He sees his friends as demons. Demons that need to be killed.

But, that's not what the movie is about.

Here's the problem with DROPPING EVIL. At the end of the movie they have a trailer for a sequel. The sequel takes everything we have learned in the first film and turns it on its ear. And I mean that in a good way. Unfortunately, it is so good that to discuss it before you watch the movie would ruin it for any viewer.

So, that's all you get.

I can say that the ping pong battle using an axe as the ball and a stool and a car door as the paddles was pretty innovative. The lead girl annoyed the Hell out of me for some reason. The box promises you Fred Williamson, which is fine, but unnecessary. Edwin Neal is in the flick, but the part is pretty mundane so, who cares? Tiffany Shepis is always a sight for this reviewer's over worked eyes and naked Tiffany Shepis is even better. Although, I prefer her posterior to her boobies, but it's still nice.

So, DROPPING EVIL is a film about teens going into the woods and one of them losing it and slaughtering the rest.

Or is it?

See, this is the part that annoys me because anything else truly would ruin it for you. Let me leave you with this. Watch the movie, the entire movie. Make sure you watch the trailer for the sequel immediately after watching the film. DO NOT WAIT! Then what is revealed to you is magnificent. All dialogue is important and makes it such an interesting film. Probably one of the most original things I have ever seen come out of the low budget arena in years.

Imagine if David Lynch had made CABIN IN THE WOODS. There! That should do it.

Have fun. I did. – *Douglas A. Waltz*

ZOMBIE BABIES (2012/IE)

I've always disliked babies. And for one reason or another, few people share my stance. This is especially true among my child-bearing friends. They're particularly unhappy when I preach my idea of government-regulated child birth in the United States. I'll say it: all potential parents should be required to pass a reading test.

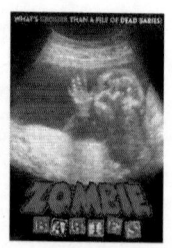

Anyway, I hate babies almost as much as I hate this ironic zombie craze, but I was willing to overlook that as long as I got a chance to boo those idiot rugrats in the subtly titled ZOMBIE BABIES. It's a movie that asks, "Is it enough to just make abortion jokes or do they need to be funny, too?"

Look, there's a lot of abortion jokes in this flick. In fact, the movie is about a man running an amateur abortion clinic. It seems that the Planned Parenthoods of the country have been monopolizing the dead fetus market and Burt is in dire need to spruce up business with a new gimmick. He decides to stage an abortion-a-thon (or abort-a-thon, I guess) for three couples: a weekend retreat of poking coat-hangers and alcohol relaxation to regroup from the sudden loss of infants.

Unfortunately, some of that moonshine they have a-brewin' is toxic enough to revitalize the pile of dead babies in the cellar. The babies, who now take a rubbery GHOULIES-like appearance, start murdering off their pro-choice parents. And these babies do away with them all: the prostitute, the homecoming queen and the overweight guy.

If you're wondering why there's an overweight guy in this film, it's so ZOMBIE BABIES can fulfill its required amount of shit jokes. Spoiler alert: the guy dies on the toilet while he's naming each of his feces pieces after characters from THE COSBY SHOW

The rest of the jokes are on par with that one. Most don't give a knee-jerk laugh reaction, but to be honest, the film's abortion theme carries it through the hour or so. The idea of rouge abortionists battling babies (especially the "giant" one) with coat hangers is a novel, perverse pleasure. I wouldn't watch it to cure my depression, but I wouldn't not watch it either... or something.

So "Is it enough to just make abortion jokes or do they need to be funny, too?" In the case of ZOMBIE BABIES, you can overlook the lack of laughs thanks to the rest of the film's originality.

Take ZOMBIE BABIES out for a stroll, but feel free to leave it on someone's doorstep. – *Jonathan Plombon*

COP IN DRAG (1984/Mya)

There are 11 movies in the Nico Giraldi series. Prior to viewing Mya's baffling DVD release of the last entry, COP IN DRAG, I had only seen the first three. Starting with COP IN BLUE JEANS, the series was hugely popular in Italy, providing the perfect milieu for Tomas Milian's knack for comedy and tough action. A Giraldi movie guaranteed some crazy stunts and action scenes and quirky (in English dubbed translation) humor. But over the course of its 11 film run, the quality of the entries deteriorated.

COP IN BLUE JEANS was a damn near perfect Milian vehicle: scope photography, outrageous acrobatic fight scenes, stuntwork and car chases, Jack Palance cashing in by playing the villain, rather quirky humor from Milian via the English dubbing supervised by Nick Alexander and his crew, with the dependable Edward Mannix dubbing Milian's voice. Giraldi himself was a campy expansion on Milian's "Rambo" in SYNDICATE SADISTS, with elements inspired by Pacino's Frank Serpico, and Robert Blake's Baretta (and Giraldi''s apartment sported a Serpico poster). Giraldi is a plainclothes police inspector who never plays by the rules. Basically a superb balance of comic and action elements long before America went crazy with buddy cop action comedies.

But later films deteriorated into cheaper, less violent entries, with Giraldi sporting bizarre eyeliner, jheri-curled hair and what can be politely described as dissolving the "exportable" elements of the movies. COP IN DRAG is the sad omega. Inspired by William Friedkin's CRUISING, LA CAGE AUX FOLLES and possibly the extended drag queen elements of later Blake Edwards comedies like VICTOR/VICTORIA, Giraldi goes undercover with another officer (conveniently, a transvestite) as a gay couple to catch a killer. What follows are dull drag queen musical numbers, plenty of queer humor, gags involving Nico's new baby and shrewish wife (in the early films, he was a womanizer, so I guess he was married in a later film) and a shocking lack of action.

The only chase scene is a listless chariot chase that leads to nothing. Seriously, nothing happens of any consequence whatsoever. The murder mystery seems rather marginal amongst seemingly endless drag queen numbers and a breakdancing musical sequence. Apparently, the spinal crunching dance form was rather popular in Italy in 1984. There is the "Batman Solution" finale between Giraldi and the villain, and very little conflict or suspense.

Milian was said by some (like Maurizio Merli) to be a pain to work with, so I wonder if this film's low quality is due to some contractual obligation or if there was enough of an audience to justify its production. If you need hints of Milian's difficult personality, check out his interview on the Blue Underground RUN MAN RUN DVD where he seems to believe he is a living incarnation of Che Guevera and displays an ego that James Lipton couldn't contain. There are a few comedic highlights, including what may be the first use of the phrase "Californication." Somebody tell the Red Hot Chili Peppers to leave that David Duchovny show alone!

Mya's disc is about as good as expected, as Italian movies of the 80s often featured television series-level production values. They must have thought this would be a staple in Gay & Lesbian sections of video stores instead of Cult or Foreign, but are there enough video stores out there to justify this getting a release before the superior preceding films?

An interesting fact was given to me by writer and filmmaker Darryl Pestilence, who has decades of experience in collecting international home video versions: "It is interesting to note that the English-language export version of A COP IN DRAG adds footage from a Luc Merenda film (from either one of his Stelvio Massi or Sergio Martino Poliziotteschi) at the start of the film and tries to present Merenda as Milian. They also recycle a fight from A COP IN BLUE JEANS to beef up the action content. No doubt they did this to help secure a few international sales (namely, Greece). The Italian print is pretty action-free, though the cat food gag and Giraldi's R-rated lullaby to his son are stand out moments."

So even the distributor knew it would have problems selling outside of Italy. But if you've always wanted to see "Serpico trapped in LA CAGE AUX FOLLES," COP IN DRAG may be your DVD cup of frappucino. – *John Grace*

WHERE THE DEAD GO TO DIE
(2011/Unearthed Films)

Don't judge WHERE THE DEAD GO TO DIE by its pseudo-cerebral dumbass of a title. That wouldn't be giving it a fair shot. You should judge WHERE THE DEAD GO TO DIE by the contents of the film. Which, actually, is as bad as the title. You can't win with this one.

WHERE THE DEAD GO TO DIE promises "90 minutes of pure mind-melting insanity." Replace "melting" with "numbing" and you'll probably have a more accurate description. It's a long, psychedelic bon voyage into tedium, an exercise in staying awake after you've endured the same animated hellfire for what you'll conclude to be forever. If anything, WHERE THE DEAD GO TO DIE may force you to realize that you have a greater purpose in life than sitting on your ass and watching WHERE THE DEAD GO TO DIE.

So, I guess it's not all bad.

WHERE THE DEAD GO TO DIE, or what I like to call WHERE TIME CEASES TO PASS, is an animated feature about a talking dog named Labby who interferes in the lives of children. According to the DVD packaging, Labby hauls these children along on "hell rides" between dimensions and time periods. This amounts to "cutting edge" seizures prompted by images of children humping dogs. Edgy.

The story drifts from one character to another. It's like SLACKER for people who wear pentagram t-shirts. And WHERE THE DEAD GO TO DIE begins feverishly with a young boy named Tommy abducting a fetus from his mother's womb after he slaughters her. From there the movie profiles a man rambling on about how he's trying to find the essence of death by warping into the minds of others. Somewhere among all this is a prostitute who is savagely consumed by a customer who wears prosthetic legs.

It's not all heartless shock. WHERE THE DEAD GO TO DIE incorporates a love story set in the tender, innocent realm of adolescence as a disfigured boy called Ralph deals with his first heartbreak. In a realistic and empathetic twist that we can all relate to, Ralph finds out that the girl he likes involuntarily stars in her father's child porn films. Confronted with a rather complicated situation, Ralph abides by a Satanic dog's advice and has sex with her while her father tapes it.

It all feels like one of those films that people probably claim to have written under the influence but it's more like one of those films that people claim to have written under the influence but really they've just written a movie that's supposed to appear like of those films that people claim to have written under the influence. In other words, it's wacky. But, to be fair, the plot moves smoother than the animation.

Director Jimmy Screamerclauz (which I believe is German) has enough material for 20 or 30 "intense minutes." It's unfortunate that it lasts about an hour longer than that. It's not that all the content is God-awful or the idea is horrible. The sea of eyes, the Cyclopes, and the bizarre worm-like creature at the bottom of the well all provide wonderfully creepy and vile vibes. It's just disappointing that you get so much of it.

It's not good, but there's something here that can be salvaged. Screamerclauz shows a bit of ambition and talent. And with some tweaking, he could manage a downright delightful piece of filth. But this isn't it. It's not WHERE THE DEAD GO TO DIE. It's just where the viewers go to sleep. – Jonathan Plombon

TRIPPIN' (2011/Camp Motion Pictures)

The older I get the more bitter I get. I used to have reasons. Now I just hate things to hate things. Who cares if my explanation is asinine? I review "scream queen" exercising DVDs, give it a positive review, and, somehow, I'm still allowed to spew my opinion for a website or zine on whether or not something's "good."

So I, being the respectable reviewer of THE NAUGHTY NOVELIST (see the ER website), went into TRIPPIN' completely closed-minded. Why? I grew weary the second I read the tagline about TRIPPIN' being a "bloodier THE BIG CHILL for a Kevin Smith generation." Kevin Smith generation? Piss off. Who says that?

I apologize. It's just that some movies are good and some of them are TRIPPIN'.

For those wondering, TRIPPIN' is about six friends who venture to a cabin secluded in the middle of nowhere. Keeping with the theme of the title, four of the idiots indulge in recreational drugs. The other two fill the roles of the straight-laced guy and straight-laced guy's prude girlfriend. Her name is Jizz. Jizz spends much of her time complaining and getting on everyone's nerves while the others spend much of their time complaining about how much they hate Jizz and how Jizz is getting on everyone else's nerves.

Oh, and people start getting hurt and in some cases, dying.

I admit that I don't know what a "Kevin Smith generation" is, but I can totally tell that this is part of it. In other words, you won't believe just how much talking there is in this film.

SPOILER ALERT: Here's some TRIPPIN' dialog:

"It's angina," the prude girlfriend responds when asked about her heart condition.

"Hehehehe, angina," stoner dumbass Zed says.

But TRIPPIN' wears on you. Sure, it's dialogue-heavy. And, sure, this is an actual line of that dialogue: "So what's up with him? Is he still in the joint?," Zed says while smoking a joint. And speaking of Zed, he's an annoying pothead Jeff Spicoli wannabe, an all-around Cody from STEP BY STEP moron doofus as contrived and stupid as Officially Licensed Jar-Jar Binks Deadhead Rolling Paper.

It does get better. Some fun begins when the small amount of blood starts to leak. The "wit" of the dialogue sometimes makes fun of itself and provides a fun running narrative of tension for the characters. Their babbling turns into more than just yapping. It becomes a symptom of their paranoia and fear. Plus, the intriguing ending makes you wonder why the rest of the movie couldn't keep up.

So, ultimately, who knows if my opinion should be heeded. But if you do take one from me, sit through the first forty minutes and you'll find something okay.

I guess. – *Jonathan Plombon*

MOLD! (2012/MVD)

It's 1984 and the war on drugs is in full swing. In a desert compound scientists are working on the one thing that will wipe out drugs once and for all. MOLD! It's a special strain commonly known as Death Mold. A contingent from the government and the military are there to see a demonstration.

They get more than they bargained for. A secret group wants a better demonstration on how it works on people.

Showtime!

MOLD! touts itself as a throwback to the gore fests of the 80s. I see that. There's a lot of gore and slime spewing throughout the flick. The producers are geniuses in that most of the action takes place at the compound where they developed the mold so we really just get to see three rooms and a hallway.

Since the complex goes into quarantine mode we get just a handful of actors as well. Pure, micro-budget production genius at its finest.

I do get that vibe of other low-budget gorefests from back in the day. Does it remind me of STREET TRASH like the back cover says? Yeah, a little. THE STUFF? No, not at all. NIGHT OF THE CREEPS? Again, a little.

It reminds me more of the no-budget stuff from the Alternative Cinema of the 90s more than anything else. This is not a dig. I really like those movies. It's like those without the naked girls. We get one girl, Ardis Campbell who has done this and dramatic recreations for the film MAN ON WIRE (2008). The concept used to get her out of most of her clothes actually made me laugh out loud.

This is your basic "mindless thing on a rampage in a scientific complex that must be defeated" scenario. It does an admirable job of getting that across. I really liked the final credits as they were all out takes from the film so we get to see funny stuff like an axe-wielding mold zombie singing Phil Collins songs. Funny stuff.

The whole film has that feel of people making a fun little flick and having fun doing it.

MOLD!

More people should pay attention to this little production company. They got it right the first time.

The disc has trailers for other films being released by Wild Eye Releasing, a director's commentary and a fun, behind-the-scenes featurette that told me I was right about how much fun they were having.

One last thing – the cover sucks. They made it look like some post-apocalyptic weird zombie thingie. It's not. The insert inside the DVD box had a much better piece of artwork they should have used instead. – *Douglas A. Waltz*

DOCUMENT OF THE DEAD
(1985/Synapse Films)

Roy Frumkes' DOCUMENT OF THE DEAD chronicles the making of George A. Romero's landmark horror classic DAWN OF THE DEAD as well as provides an insightful look into the filmmaking technique and motivations behind NIGHT OF THE LIVING DEAD, MARTIN and even DAY OF THE DEAD.

The focus is, however, primarily on DAWN OF THE DEAD which suits me fine as DAWN OF THE DEAD is my all-time favorite horror film and quite possibly my all-time favorite genre film period. With DOTD, Romero illustrated the potential for addressing political and social issues within the realm of genre and how you can do so without being preachy about it. Through the many interviews Frumkes conducts with Romero throughout the course of filming, you really do get into the head of Romero and how he believes through exaggerated metaphors, horror can rise above the silliness it's all too often associated with and really stand for something more.

There are many things about DOCUMENT OF THE DEAD that I admire. For starters, the fact that this was shot on actual film is astounding. Nowadays, you wouldn't even imagine shooting a documentary on anything but HD, where concerns of limitations of space and availability of stock are non-existent. I can only imagine the anxiety Frumkes and company must have had while conducting an interview with Romero, fearing that they would run out of film at a particular moment of interest and be unable to capture it.

I also love the fact that this is one of the very few pieces on Romero that actually treats the man as an auteur filmmaker who has something to say, as opposed to the "zombie guy," a title he's unfortunately saddled with by other magazines, websites, documentaries, etc.

My main critique of the film would be that while it's interesting to hear from Romero, Savini and others involved in DAWN OF THE DEAD, the documentary unfortunately comes across as a very dry talking heads piece. I would have much preferred the cinema verite approach, where they would have simply followed these guys around like a fly on the wall where we feel like we're part of the crew making this film. There's a very academic-sounding voiceover that plagues most of the piece where we're introduced to "Director George A. Romero" or "Special Effects Artist Tom Savini." Hearing everyone identified by their name and title each and every time they appear on camera gets old fast and it often made me feel like I was watching one of those especially boring educational documentaries made by the National Film Board of Canada.

So on the whole, DOCUMENTARY OF THE DEAD is fascinating in that when you really stop to think about it, this may very well be the first "making of" an independent feature film, so from a novelty standpoint, it's worth checking out. But on the other hand, its heavy-handed educational approach makes for a very dry viewing experience. – *Matthew Saliba*

THE BIG GUNDOWN
(1966/Grindhouse Releasing)

Grindhouse Releasing proudly places another stellar collector's edition directly into the insatiable mitts of cult cinema fans, this time resplendent with the grim visage of a well-seasoned Lee Van Cleef and a roguish Tomas Milian. The beautiful slipcover boasts this to be "The Ultimate Spaghetti Western", and to match this braggadocious claim, Grindhouse Releasing has packed an epic four discs into the set. Are they betting good money after bad, or is this the superb film which the packaging and deep cuts purport it to be?

Right out of the gate the presence of Lee Van Cleef means you should pay special attention to this Sergio Sollima-directed epic. His sun burnished face and squinty demeanor belies a dry, sardonic wit, combining to form the quintessential Spaghetti Western protagonist every time he saddles up. Here he plays the legendary bounty hunter, 'Colorado' Corbitt, a ruthlessly efficient hunter of men who still possesses a civilized sense of fair play. That may be the sort of sentimentality which could get a lesser man killed, but Corbitt is so skilled that he merely takes each setback in stride like a gunslinging Zen master. While being solicited into collaboration with a railroad tycoon in exchange for the funds he needs to parlay his popularity into a run for higher office, Corbitt is tasked with tracking Cuchillo, an outlaw who stands accused of raping and murdering a little girl.

Into that potentially grim role steps rugged European star Tomas Milian (star of DJANGO KILL...IF YOU LIVE, SHOOT and FACE TO FACE), who has a tremendous amount of fun playing a cat and mouse game with Van Cleef across visually stunning backdrops, and through a great number of often humorous encounters. Back and forth swings the pendulum of advantage as these rivals traverse a series of Wild West set pieces, most of which are resoundingly enjoyable. However, one overly long sequence – depicting a ranch matron and her harem of cowboys – feels clunky, out of place, and just plain disjointed when viewed alongside the rest of the picture. This strange allegorical side-quest would more suitably fit among the adventures of Odysseus than the campfire stories of Van Cleef. Still, it only accounts for a small portion of the movie and doesn't cataclysmically derail this imaginative, giddy and visually resplendent Spaghetti Western.

THE BIG GUNDOWN features a memorably forceful score by Ennio Morricone, whom any Spaghetti Western fan worth their side iron will be familiar with thanks to his work on Sergio Leone's *Dollars Trilogy*. Here Morricone is much more brazen, exposing his horns to perhaps the sassy influence of the then wildly popular James Bond series. Indeed this film opens with a brightly colored montage of stills as Morricone's sultry theme "Run, Man, Run" rocks the boat of expectations. Belted out by singer Maria Cristina Brancucci, whose range is powerful and impressive, this tune will get stuck in your head, and Morricone hammers that home by layering upon this track to build most of the score. Grindhouse Releasing saw fit to gift collectors with the *entire* original film score on its own separate CD, which just forms the tip of the special features iceberg.

This generous collector's edition contains the 95 minute expanded U.S. cut, which from a pacing standpoint feels like the strongest presentation of the film, on both Blu-Ray and DVD. It also offers the extended director's cut, in Italian with English subtitles, which clocks in with a whopping fifteen extra minutes restored, on its own separate Blu-ray Disc. Interviews featured include director Sergio Sollima (FACE TO FACE), star Tomas Milian and writer Sergio Donati; and the audio commentary is a trivia-rich gold mine thanks to western film experts C. Courtney Joyner and Henry C. Parke (who also did a bang up commentary on Blue Underground's release of Van Cleef's GRAND DUEL). The transfer here is a new 2K digital restoration, which offers superb clarity as the camera soaks in the gorgeous scenescapes. Still galleries, trailers, and TV spots round out this deep release, with a rich liner note contribution from the aforementioned Joyner.

When the pistols run dry and the gun smoke settles, Grindhouse Releasing's treatment of THE BIG GUNDOWN stands as the high water mark toward which all other genre caretakers should shoot. Add this one to the collection now, before it rides off into the out of print sunset. – *Chuck Francisco*

EMPIRE OF THE APES (2013/MVD)

I'm a lifelong, card-carrying PLANET OF THE APES lover – but I'm not what you would call an APES "purist". Whether we're talking original pentalogy, black & white Marvel magazine, 1970s TV show, Power Records LPs, 90s comic or Fiammetta Flamini's 1984 single "Fuoco Fuoco", I'm pretty much all in when it comes to POTA in pop culture. (You'll notice the Tim Burton film is conspicuous by its absence.)

This love of (almost) all things APE even extends to such seemingly ill-advised efforts as the Japanese movie TIME OF THE APES in which two schoolchildren take refuge from an earthquake while visiting their uncle's hi-tech lab, only to wake up in a world run by apes who dress like Colonel Sanders and drive American muscle cars. (See dantenet.com for our full review.) Edited down to 98 minutes from 26 (!) television episodes, TIME OF THE APES manages to be simultaneously charming and perplexing.

To this unofficial APES cannon you can also add EMPIRE OF THE APES, an insanely low-budget but completely entertaining riff on the genre written and directed by Mark Polonia (best known for horror films like SPLATTER FARM and SPLATTER BEACH made with brother John) featuring special effects from Brett Piper (THEY BITE) and Anthony Polonia.

Theel (Elizabeth Costanzo), Jada (Marie DeLorenzo) and Dane (Danielle Donahue) are prisoners on a transport ship piloted by Captain Zantor (Steve Diasparra). Rather than spend life as "a love slave to a three-headed onion" the trio bust out of their cell and commandeer an escape pod with Zantor in hot pursuit. Landing on a planet of the apes – 'natch – the trio squabble and blurt lines like "I won't let one of those beasts take me!" as they attempt to survive their captivity, avoid being returned to Zantor or used as part of the apes' "aggressive reproduction campaign". All while wearing workout gear or denim shorts.

To be frank, I'm probably overstating things by referring to it as a "planet of the apes". It's more like a "campground of the apes" since it's apparently populated by: Korg, the elder (Ken Van Sant); warrior Baal (James Carolus); pacifist Trask (Jeff Kirkendall); and, a handful of other dudes in stiff, clunky ape masks.

Sure, it'd be easy to blast EMPIRE for the veneer of cheapness it wears (almost defiantly) on its sleeve, the costuming, the ape masks that barely move and the fact that even at 79 minutes the thing starts to feel a bit padded. But I'll be damned if I didn't have a lot of fun with it thanks to dialogue like "Your negligence denied me of my prize! Fight Baal or taste the energy gun!" and "Tell me feisty one… how did you come to our Garden of Eden?". Polonia even throws in a handful of nods to the original POTA flicks and embraces the concept's beastly sexuality (something the original series seemed to shy away from), even staging "The Great Ape Games" with the prisoners as prizes.

I'm not going to lie to you. I'm more excited for REVOLT OF THE EMPIRE OF THE APES (the sequel teased in the end credits) than I am for DAWN OF THE PLANET OF THE APES. – Dan Taylor

42ND STREET FOREVER: THE PEEP SHOW COLLECTION VOL. 1 (2013/ Impulse Pictures)

In the age before cellphones and share buttons within every app, there was still short burst porn, ready to satisfy the needs of any viewer looking for a quick, cheap and dirty thrill. Several DVD labels have been putting together 8mm loop collections, and Impulse Pictures has joined the party by bringing the 42ND STREET FOREVER series into a new direction with THE PEEP SHOW COLLECTION.

Personally, I love the loops and that lone whirring projector sound playing over various and sundry sex sequences from days gone by. It taps into an experience that I never personally had, growing up in the age of VHS and getting my first job in a video shop so that I could rent all those tapes from "THE BLACK BOOK" or behind the red curtain of mystery, just beyond the "Horror" section. This collection feels like what it must have been like to sneak in some alone time with pornography, the way it was when you could either be a housewife that would face a hopeful interruption from a vacuum cleaner salesman or wonder what your secretary was getting up to in the ladies room during her break!

While the flicks are cheap, sometimes nasty, occasionally funny and usually brief, Impulse has put some serious stroke into the production by including some big names in porn in early appearances worth watching for. While the box will remind you that these are "re-mastered in high definition from original film prints" don't think you are in for more than a scratchy good time, and that is all for the better.

For a second I actually feared that they would look *too* clean! Never fear, this is the dirty deeds you wanted to see and they still look dirty (and are all the tastier for it).

Included are 15 loops that veer all over the place from the sexy and simple ("Sheep Weren't Never Like This", "Afternoon Dildo Party") to stranger domestic distressing goings on ("Come On My Eggs"), right up to the timeless women-in-prison drama where a little behind bars box munching turns into a spanking and power wielding blowjob micro movie ("Jailhouse Fuck").

Definitely showing all sides of porn, Impulse provides one hell of a debut volume that shows while there is lots of innocence in these early porn productions, they also had a wide range of tone and configurations, just like the sexuality of their intended customer. And you NEVER know what you'll see next, as best exemplified by the sudden title being clear in "The Spice Of Life" when we have full-on water sports (right down to the penile tip shake-off in the gullet). Well, I didn't see that coming!

But for the porn fans that enjoy the early looks, John Holmes – looking large as ever – has two appearances. First is the noirish (OK, not really) "It Takes A Thief" that features The Sultan of Schlong busting in on a woman masturbating and forcing (ahem) her to take all of him at gunpoint. It probably helps that she seems completely oblivious to the faux "forced" angle and does her job with great vigor. I couldn't stop laughing that the masked Holmes hair was reminiscent of Norman Osborn's 70s hairdo in Marvel's *The Amazing Spider-Man*. Weird! He rises again in "Deeper Throat" in a stunning display of oral skill from his unnamed female partner. And again ... Harry Osborn hair! You can also find Annie Sprinkle not sprinkling in a straight ahead sex scene, as well as Lisa DeLeeuw (one of this reviewer's favorites) in an outstanding bit of biz called "One Hung Low." I'm not sure I get the title on this one, but who cares?

Group sex, dudes and gals smiling and fucking, nurses getting it on and so much more. It's raunch and roll from a generation (or two...) gone by. If you are interested, you'll be satisfied by this installment and look forward to many more!

The disc gives you the chance to sit back for two hours of uninterrupted projection or you can drop your virtual coin and enjoy each one again and again, depending upon your mood. And a MegaBoner bonus goes to having the legendary Robin Bougie of CINEMA SEWER fame provide liner notes on the loops and other material enclosed in this volume. So, drop your pants, click 'Play' and be sure to wipe up the booth for the next patron! 42ND STREET FOREVER: THE PEEP SHOW COLLECTION VOLUME 1 will give you a chance to be your own private jizz mopper in the comfort of your own home! – David Zuzelo

HANDS OF THE RIPPER
(1971/Synapse Films)

HANDS OF THE RIPPER occupies a precarious place in the waning years of Hammer's decline as a powerhouse of period horror. Yet recent nostalgic interest, coupled with lovingly jam packed Blu-Ray releases by genre houses, have yielded increased reverence and respect for formerly discarded "lesser" titles from the Hammer catalogue. As a long time admirer of HANDS OF THE RIPPER, I was immensely pleased at the opportunity a fresh release from attentive studio Synapse Films represented. The story takes the well-worn Jack the Ripper mythos and gussies it up in the trappings of a gothic thriller, replete with sequences of such horrific gore that they had to be trimmed for the American release (the hand mirror-becomes-dagger is a wickedly stylish favorite of mine).

As an infant, Anna witnesses the brutal murder of her mother by her father – the infamous Jack the Ripper – when the former discovers blood all over her husband's hands. From there life is quite unkind to the girl as she grows up under the roof of a shyster medium and would-be pimp, Madame Bullard. Anna, now fully grown and played by the cute as a button Angharad Rees, is mere seconds from her first jaunt down prostitution lane when environmental factors trigger within her a murderous outbreak which her slight physicality suggests should be impossible. Is her homicidal power rooted in psychological ailment or in a supernatural link to her wicked father? Determined to discover the truth is Dr. Prichard (played by the extremely talented Eric

ER #52 :: page 63

Porter), who takes custody of Anna in an attempt to psychoanalyze her in the vein of the then-trendy Sigmund Freud.

There's an old school dynamic at play here which many young horror fans may not be accustomed to. By assigning the older Dr. Prichard as our protagonist, a link is established to classic films which positioned the learned, older male as the character we empathize with. As in Hammer's own THE PLAGUE OF THE ZOMBIES (1966), the hero is an older man of the established patriarchy, placing him above criminal suspicion and allowing him to act with agency in the pursuit of the truth. Hammer was able to maintain this structure for longer than contemporaries since their movies were period pieces, occurring during eras when this was the expected norm. Considering the situation in hindsight, this methodology may have led to the studio's downfall as horror movies trended toward positioning teenagers or young adults in the role of protagonist. But in this film it comes off as a brilliant shuffle of focus, evoking a unique series of interesting situations which have long fallen out of favor in modern horror cinema. In essence, HANDS OF THE RIPPER feels fresh because of its lost, antiquated ways.

Visually HANDS OF THE RIPPER comes equipped with all of the lush gothic trappings to which Hammer fans are accustomed. Outdoor scenes set among London's Edwardian cobblestone lanes act as an inescapable time warp, despite being filmed on the backlots of Pinewood Studios. Blood is unnaturally vivid as it's let loose from its arterial prison to spray haphazardly across Anna's regal dresses. Rees' transformation from innocent and adorable to cold and vicious lives in the fractured facial contortions which wrack her normally lovely countenance. The film transfer by Synapse Films is top-notch, choosing to go with a grainier texture which accentuates the late night nature of this type of film. It's warm, it's familiar and it's appealing to the nostalgia center of the brain.

Special features aimed at pleasing genre fans are baked into this combo release (both DVD and Blu-Ray are included). The highlight is a newly-crafted feature by renowned production company Ballyhoo Motion Pictures, which includes excerpts of an audio interview with Angharad Rees from 2012, shortly prior to her passing. Also included is a still motion gallery which visually chronicles the breadth of Hammer gore.

Expect HANDS OF THE RIPPER appreciation to grow in the near future, thanks largely to this stellar release from Synapse, who took special care of the transfer and made it readily available for a new generation. This edition belongs in the collection of all serious Hammer fans and anyone looking for beautiful trappings to comfortably embrace the hot splash of life's blood upon the floor. – *Chuck Francisco*

Printed in Great Britain
by Amazon.co.uk, Ltd.,
Marston Gate.